BrightRED PUBLISHING

BrightRED Results

LEARN TO WRITE

for Curriculum for Excellence

Dr Christopher Nicol

First published in 2015 by:
Bright Red Publishing Ltd
1 Torphichen Street
Edinburgh
EH3 8HX

A CIP record for this book is available from the British Library

ISBN 978-1-906736-74-3

With thanks to:
PDQ Digital Media Solutions Ltd (layout), Sue Moody, Bright Writing Ltd. (edit)

Cover design and series book design by Caleb Rutherford – e i d e t i c

Acknowledgements
Every effort has been made to seek all copyright holders. If any have been overlooked, then Bright Red Publishing will be delighted to make the necessary arrangements.

Permission has been sought from all relevant copyright holders and Bright Red Publishing are grateful for the use of the following:

monkeybusinessimages/iStock.com (p 5); FrankRamspott/iStock.com (p 5); Caleb Rutherford e i d e t i c (p 6); rashch/iStock.com (p 9); Caleb Rutherford e i d e t i c (p 9); Palto/Dreamstime.com (p 11); tusumaru/iStock.com (p 13); An extract from 'Trieste and the Meaning of Nowhere' by Jan Morris, published by Faber & Faber 2001 (p 14); Image licensed by Ingram Image (p 16); fourohfour/iStock.com (p 17); An extract from Rude, Carolyn D.: Dragga, SAM,Technical Editing, 3rd Ed. © 2002, p 51. Reprinted by permission of Pearson Education, Inc., New York (p 19); Caleb Rutherford e i d e t i c (p 20); Image licensed by Ingram Image (p 20); Image licensed by Ingram Image (p 22); dk_photos/iStock.com (p 23); Anton_Soklov/iStock.com (p 24); Caleb Rutherford e i d e t i c (pp 26 to 27); Caleb Rutherford e i d e t i c (p 27); Lonely_/iStock.com (p 28); Davide Guglielmo/freeimages.com, Caleb Rutherford e i d e t i c (p 29); An extract from 'Lanark' by Alasdair Gray, published by Canongate Books Ltd 1981 (p 34); An extract from 'Souls Belated' by Edith Wharton, published 1899 (public domain) (p 35); AndreyPopov/iStock.com (p 36); An extract from 'Better Business Writing' by Timothy R.V. Foster published by Kogan Page 2002 © Timothy R.V. Foster/AdSlogans (p 37); prill/iStock.com (p 38); iSebastian/iStock.com (p 40); ZU_09/iStock.com (p 41); Pyroe/iStock.com (p 41); duncan1890/iStock.com (p 41); Caleb Rutherford e i d e t i c (p 44); Caleb Rutherford e i d e t i c (p 45); DNHanlon/iStock.com (p 46); Anatollii Babii/iStock.com (p 47); Maria Li/freeimages.com (p 47); rawartitsmedia (CC BY-ND 2.0 http://creativecommons.org/licenses/by-nd/2.0/); NTNU Trodheim (CC BY-SA 2.0 https://creativecommons.org/licenses/by-sa/2.0/); David Robert Bliwass (CC BY 2.0 http://creativecommons.org/licenses/by/2.0/) (p 51); An extract from 'Of Mice and Men' by John Steinbeck, published by Covici Friede 1937 © The Estate of John Steinbeck (p 51); Rawpixel Ltd/iStock.com (p 52); 4774344sean/iStock.com (p 52); Image licensed by Ingram Image (p 54); An extract from 'Night Pillow' by Hugh C. Rae, published by Viking/Penguin Books Ltd 1969 (p 55); An extract from 'Atonement' by Ian McEwan, published by Anchor Books, a division of Random House Inc., New York 2001 (p 55); joelblit/iStock.com (p 56); Caleb Rutherford (p 57); Choreograph/iStock.com (p 58); Tpopova/iStock.com (p 59); QUAYSIDE/iStock.com (p 60); yaruta/iStock.com (p 61); Image licensed by Ingram Image (p 61); tibofox/iStock.com (p 62); AlexKalina/iStock.com (p 62); An extract from 'Paris to the Past' by Ina Caro, published by W.W. Norton & Company, Inc. 2011 (p 64); vgajic/iStock.com (p 65); lisa fx/iStock.com (p 65); The article 'There's no point wearing a poppy if you just want to be popular' by David Mitchell, taken from theguardian.com, 17 November 2013. Copyright Guardian News & Media Ltd 2013 (p 67); verdateo/iStock.com (p 68); Caleb Rutherford e i d e t i c (p 71); timchen/iStock.com (p 74); danielle71/iStock.com (p 75); zimmytws/iStock.com (p 76); LudovicaBastianini/iStock.com (p 78); Liuser/iStock.com (p 80); pablographix/iStock.com (p 80); Caleb Rutherford e i d e t i c (p 83); Caleb Rutherford e i d e t i c (p 86); cirodelia/iStock.com (p 88); An extract from N5 English Specimen Question Paper Critical Reading p27 © Scottish Qualifications Authority (n.b. solutions do not emanate from the SQA) (p 88); Image licensed by Ingram Image (p 91); AnaBGD/iStock.com (p 92).

Printed and bound in the UK by Charlesworth Press.

CONTENTS LIST

> *We are all apprentices in a craft where no one ever becomes a master.* – Ernest Hemingway

DEVELOPING SUCCESSFUL WRITING SKILLS

Developing successful writing skills can be a lifelong journey. You are now at the point in your journey where you are approaching the milestones of the Nationals and Higher English. Use this book as your travel guide. Use it to polish and develop your writing skills **now** – before you get anywhere near your exams. This will not only boost your competence, but your self-confidence too.

So, where do we start?

GETTING THE BASICS RIGHT

To ensure exam success, you need to get the basics right – things that you have been learning about ever since you started writing, but about which you still have niggling questions, such as: where exactly do I use commas? When do I use who's or whose? What is it my teacher says about 'i before e' in awkward words?

IMPROVING YOUR EXPRESSION

You also need to think about expressing your ideas in a way that does full justice to them – for example: what kind of sentence structure should I use to achieve a particular effect? How can I develop my vocabulary?

WRITING BETTER ESSAYS

Once you've thought about the basics and expression, you then need to think about the conventions of the various genres in which you'll be asked to write – for example: what are sensible guidelines for each genre? How do I go about applying them to my own ideas?

Always remember, however, that there is no one 'right' way of writing an essay – no matter what genre you choose. Good writing is not about obeying someone else's rules. It is about freeing up your ability to do full justice to your thinking. And to do that, it's a good idea to look at successful, published writing to see what you can learn from it.

What you'll find in this Guide are some tried-and-tested approaches to the writing process to help you find your own way forward.

SHARING AND DISCUSSING

When you get to the sections that deal with the creating of your own texts, you'll find that we often suggest getting your work reviewed by a partner. By discussing openly with someone engaged in a similar process, you'll discover that shared experience and constructive comments can help you both improve your performance.

PROCESS AS WELL AS PRODUCT

If you're interested enough to have invested in this Guide, then you're obviously aiming to achieve an end product that brings a top grade. But very few people are talented enough to sit down and write a first-class essay right off. Effective writing requires you to think, plan, draft and redraft until you produce the very best of which you are capable. This Guide will give you support at every stage of this process to help you achieve the result you are looking for.

GETTING THE BEST OUT OF THIS GUIDE

There's no one 'right' way of using this Guide. You could have a look at the Contents page first to see the areas we cover and then go straight to those areas where you feel you need help. Or you might want to work through the Guide, section by section – it's up to you. Whatever method you choose, make sure that you use the Guide to help you address any points that your teacher flags up in your work, so the same criticisms don't crop up again.

You'll find tips and strategies to help you develop your writing skills, and activities to help you reinforce these skills for SQA exams and for life.

Let's get going!

PUNCTUATION

He who neglects punctuation, or mispunctuates, is liable to be misunderstood. – Edgar Allan Poe

FULL STOPS AND COMMAS

THE ROLE OF PUNCTUATION

Faulty punctuation can confuse your meaning – and lose you valuable marks. Clear punctuation helps the reader to understand your meaning quickly and easily. If a reader has to struggle to make sense of the flow of your sentence – because you have been careless in your use of punctuation – the strength of your writing is seriously weakened (as are your hopes of impressing a marker)!

Before we look at the function of each of the most common punctuation marks, let's look first at the three distinct categories of punctuation and their roles:

- Punctuation that marks out the **limits** of a sentence:
  full stop   question mark   exclamation mark
- Punctuation that **shapes** the sentence within its limits:
  comma   colon   semi-colon
- Punctuation that adds **special effects** to the sentence:
  inverted commas   ellipsis   dashes and brackets

FULL STOPS

Full stops to end a sentence

Most commonly, they indicate the completion of a sentence:

> **EXAMPLE** Having finished his lunch, he left the canteen.

If another sentence is to follow, it must begin with a capital letter:

> **EXAMPLE** Having finished his lunch, he left the canteen. No one paid any attention.

Full stops in abbreviations

But we also need full stops in some abbreviations – usually the ones from Latin:

- **i.e.** ('id est' – that is to say)
- **e.g.** ('exempli gratia' – for the sake of example)
- **etc.** ('et cetera' – and the rest)

COMMAS

They may be small, but commas are the most hard-working of all the punctuation marks we use. They turn up all the time in text, fulfilling a great variety of functions, so you need to know how to use them.

+ DON'T FORGET

A good understanding of the function of punctuation marks will not only help your writing to be clearer – it can also boost your performance in Reading for Understanding, Analysis and Evaluation. Intelligent use of question marks, exclamation marks, colons and so on all have their own particular effects on the reader. Make sure you exploit these effects to the full when you write, no matter what genre.

Used well, commas are one of the more helpful punctuation items in shaping the sense of what you are trying to say and guiding the reader through your text.

Here are just some of the more common ways they can be used. You need to be familiar with all of them.

Commas in lists

Perhaps the most common use of a comma is in separating smaller items in a list. These items may be adjectives, nouns, verbs or adverbs.

EXAMPLES

Her garden was a riot of yellow, purple, pink and red blossoms. (listed adjectives)

Her favourites were poppies, lilies, carnations and roses. (listed nouns)

He swam, cycled, wrestled and trained with weights all summer. (listed verbs)

I want this done quickly, efficiently, discreetly and inexpensively. (listed adverbs)

WATCH OUT

The item before the final 'and' in such lists does **not** require a comma after it because the 'and' is already joining the items in the list. A comma would just be duplicating that join.

Commas in apposition

You use phrases in apposition almost every time you write. When we use a phrase in apposition, **two** commas are needed. A phrase in apposition adds extra information to an item, and you need a comma before **and** after it. For example:

Alison, John's twin sister, insisted on coming with us.

So 'John's twin sister' is our phrase in apposition here.

Other examples might be:

EXAMPLES

Helen Mirren, <u>one of Britain's most successful actresses,</u> stars in *Red* and *Red 2*.

Elspeth, <u>my mother's best friend</u>, is famous for her cupcakes.

Even Jamie and Darren, <u>both good swimmers,</u> found the race exhausting.

WATCH OUT

Often students put in one but not both commas. A phrase in apposition needs **two** commas, and it looks sloppy if you miss one out.

Commas before connecting words, to join two independent statements

These connecting words are often **and, but, or, so, nor, for** and **yet**.

EXAMPLES

There was no British Embassy at that time, **so** we had to go to the Swiss Consulate for our visas.

It was clearly not a government of national unity, **yet** it was something more than a mere one-party affair.

These experiments led to many interesting theories, **but** it was very difficult to prove a single one of them.

Commas in direct speech

We need to be alert to how to use commas when we are writing dialogue and addressing a person directly.

EXAMPLE

(a) 'Is this the best you can do, Fiona?'

(b) 'Fiona, is this the best you can do?'

Note that we need a comma immediately before using a person's name, as in (a). We also need it after the name if the sentence continues, as in (b).

WATCH OUT

If the person's name comes midway in the sentence, the name requires a comma before **and** after it.

EXAMPLE

'Tell me, Mr Kennedy, what exactly do you mean by that?'

THINGS TO DO AND THINK ABOUT

Go through your most recent essays to check out which punctuation marks have caught you out and use the advice here to prevent you making the same mistakes again. It's worth taking the time to get it right now – you'll know how to use punctuation correctly throughout the rest of your life.

MORE ABOUT COMMAS

COMMAS (CONTINUED)

Here are some more examples of where you should use commas.

Commas after introductory words or phrases

Think how often you start conversations with words like 'Well, ...' or 'Look, ...' or 'Listen, ...' In writing, we often begin with similar words or phrases to prepare the reader for what is to come. We use commas after these words or phrases to emphasise that there is some important information to follow.

> **EXAMPLES**
>
> On the other hand, property there is cheaper.
>
> Generally speaking, we get on quite well.
>
> For example, fares to Milan can be cheaper than those to Paris.
>
> However, this did not last.
>
> In contrast, the weather here was foul.

There are also useful words called 'attitude markers' which come at the beginning of sentences and are put there to colour our response to what we are about to hear. (These are highly useful in persuasive writing, which we shall be discussing later.) Attitude markers also need commas to separate them from the upcoming content.

> **EXAMPLES**
>
> Sadly, she burned the manuscript.
>
> Interestingly, we heard nothing of the bankruptcy.
>
> Stupidly, I forgot the compass.

Commas after introductory descriptive phrases

Introductory descriptive phrases describe the noun or noun phrase that immediately follows them. These descriptive phrases are always followed by a comma.

> **EXAMPLES**
>
> Footsore and weary, the tramp collapsed on the bench.
>
> Crystal clear, the night sky glittered overhead.
>
> Indecisive by nature, Hamlet fails to act for much of the play.

There is another type of introductory descriptive phrase called a participial phrase. A participle is a word that looks like a verb but acts like an adjective and often ends in '...ing', '...ed' and '...en'. A participial phrase consists of the participle and other words need to complete the idea begun by the participle. It usually comes before the noun or noun phrase it describes.

> **EXAMPLES**
>
> Finishing his speech, he sat down to great applause.
>
> Brushing crumbs from her dress, she ran upstairs.
>
> Plagued by gremlins, the public address system finally gave up.
>
> Dumped by his girlfriend, Hamish was a sorry sight.

AVOID THE COMMA SPLICE AT ALL COSTS!

English teachers will tell you that probably the most common mistake they spend time correcting is the 'comma splice'. Employers, too, scrutinise letters of application for this sure-fire give-away of feeble English usage.

So, what is the comma splice?

> **EXAMPLE**
>
> They spent a fortune on the house, it was meant to show off their wealth.

You can see that, while there is a strong connection in **information** and **sense** between the two statements, there is no real **grammatical** connection between the two statements. They have merely been 'spliced' together with a stray comma; they have not been joined correctly.

There are a number of ways that we can bind the two statements together much more convincingly (and correctly).

Use a full stop

These are two independent statements, so we can just treat them like that.

They spent a fortune on the house. It was meant to show off their wealth.

Each statement perhaps comes across more powerfully when given its own space.

Use a semi-colon

A semi-colon here acknowledges an interconnection in sense between two items which are better presented, grammatically, as independent statements.

> **EXAMPLE**
>
> They spent a fortune on the house; it was meant to show off their wealth.

Use a conjunction

A conjunction is a name for a word that connects other words or phrases together. Some examples are 'since', 'because' or 'as'.

> **EXAMPLE**
>
> They spent a fortune on the house <u>since</u> it was meant to show off their wealth.

Use a relative pronoun

A relative pronoun is simply a 'which', 'who' or 'whom' word.

Here, 'which' would work well.

> **EXAMPLE**
>
> They spent a fortune on the house <u>which</u> was meant to show off their wealth.

Use a participial phrase

You can use a participial phrase to join the two statements together. (If you can't remember what a participial phrase is, remind yourself by looking at the examples on the previous page.)

> **EXAMPLES**
>
> <u>Meaning to show off their wealth,</u> they spent a fortune on the house.
>
> <u>Spending a fortune on their house,</u> they meant to show off their wealth.

DON'T FORGET

If you find yourself about to use the comma splice – STOP – and think about using one of these five options. Or try changing your wording. Remember that the comma splice can spoil an otherwise good piece of work, create a bad impression of your writing and affect your grade – so don't use it. Go over our suggestions for combining statements successfully. You have many options to choose from.

THINGS TO DO AND THINK ABOUT

At first sight, the comma might seem to be a fairly insignificant mark on the page. It isn't. It plays an important role in ensuring that your reader understands your intentions clearly and easily. Get to know the many ways you can use it in your writing.

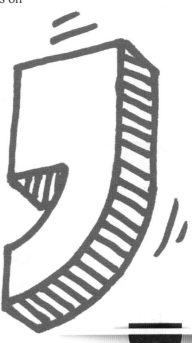

QUESTION MARKS, EXCLAMATION MARKS, APOSTROPHES AND INVERTED COMMAS

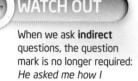

WATCH OUT

When we ask **indirect** questions, the question mark is no longer required: *He asked me how I explained that.*

DON'T FORGET

When writing a creative text, remember that a **series** of questions is often a good way of showing your character's bewilderment or panic: *Could this be true? Had she been a fool? Was this the end of the road for her?*

DON'T FORGET

Be cautious with exclamation marks – they lose their impact if they are overused.

DON'T FORGET

Avoid these abbreviations in formal letters, argumentative essays and reports. They are best used in chattier, more colloquial types of writing.

WATCH OUT

Be particularly careful with the **-'ve** words! People sometimes mishear **could've/ would've/ should've** and write **could of/would of/should of** instead. This is a big mark loser. Don't do it.

QUESTION MARKS

These are needed at the end of all **direct** questions:

EXAMPLE How do you explain that?

EXCLAMATION MARKS

These are useful when you want to show strong emotions such as surprise, anger or excitement:

EXAMPLES

So it was true! (surprise) Shut up! (anger)
A trip to Hollywood! (excitement)

They also turn up at the end of short greetings in dialogue:

EXAMPLES Hello! Hi there!

and in exclamations:

EXAMPLES Ouch! Oh no! Great!

APOSTROPHES

The two principal uses of the apostrophe are to indicate:

a) where a letter (or letters) has been omitted
b) to show possession.

Omission

We use the apostrophe here to show where a letter has been missed out. Here are some common examples of this kind of abbreviation:

EXAMPLES

I'm, you're, he's/ she's, we're, they're, I can't, I should've, I would've.

Possession (singular nouns)

In the case of singular nouns (where there is one thing or person being the 'possessor') possession is shown by placing an apostrophe between the end of the noun and an 's'.

EXAMPLES

• Madge's mother • the nation's shame • the team's coach

Possession (plural nouns)

Students sometimes get confused about plural nouns but just keep the following in mind and there shouldn't be a problem:

Identify how many people/items/possessors there are. If there's **one**, then use the technique for singular nouns.

If there's **more than one** possessor, then remember that in English the plural is often formed simply by adding an '**s**' to many nouns:

> **EXAMPLES**
>
> - The pandas
> - the McQueens
> - the twins
>
> To show possession in these cases, just add an apostrophe after the 's':
> - The pandas' enclosure
> - the McQueens' reputation
> - the twins' mother

INVERTED COMMAS

Like commas, inverted commas (or quotation marks, to give them their other name) fulfil a number of purposes.

Direct speech

You need to use quotation marks in your text to show when people begin and end speaking:

> **EXAMPLES**
>
> 'You must be the new student,' said Anna.
>
> 'Are you the new student?' asked Anna.
>
> 'You must be the new student!' Anna cried.

Whether you use a comma, a question mark or an exclamation mark here, make sure it comes **inside** the final set of inverted commas, not **outside** them.

DON'T FORGET

Direct speech always requires inverted commas to mark it out. Ordinary commas will not do the job.

WATCH OUT

Be careful with punctuation marks **before** the final inverted comma.

When you wish to interrupt the speech of your speaker – which is quite a sophisticated way to add variety to your sentences – you need to be careful again of how you punctuate this interruption.

> **EXAMPLE**
>
> 'Can you tell me,' began the teacher in a sarcastic tone, 'what this is supposed to be?'

As before, you need a comma **inside** the inverted commas before the break in dialogue. You also need one before the dialogue re-starts. The dialogue re-starts with no capital letter. Why? Because the dialogue sentence was merely interrupted, not completed.

But look at this.

> **EXAMPLE**
>
> 'Sit down, Jamie!' said the teacher in an angry tone, 'You are disturbing the whole class.'

Note the capital letter at 'You'. Why this difference? Because the teacher uttered two distinct sentences, both of which were completed, not interrupted.

Quotations

Quotations might crop up in your text even when there is no dialogue involved:

> **EXAMPLE**
>
> A spokesman for the government was 'unavailable for comment' when we contacted the department.

Irony

When writers wish to indicate that something is only 'so-called' or wish to hint they think the opposite of the words surface meaning, they often use inverted commas:

> **EXAMPLES**
>
> The 'castle' was no more than a jumped-up hotel.
>
> My 'friend' had just slammed a £60 parking fine on my windscreen.
>
> Jean's 'help' took me three days and a small fortune to put right.

TITLES

Inverted commas are also used to indicate titles of books, poems, films and songs:

> **EXAMPLES**
>
> 'Catching Fire' is a novel by Suzanne Collins.
>
> Wilfred Owen is the writer of 'Anthem for Doomed Youth'.
>
> 'Maleficent' stars Angelina Jolie.

COLONS, SEMI-COLONS, ELLIPSIS, DASHES AND BRACKETS

COLONS

Colons can be used to introduce the following:

* Additional information, explanations, elaborations and definitions

> **EXAMPLE**
>
> Life looked bleak: he had no money and Claire had broken off their engagement last week.

* Lists

> **EXAMPLE**
>
> Colons may be used for a variety of purposes: to introduce additional information; to introduce a list; to introduce a quotation or subtitle.

* Quotations

> **EXAMPLE**
>
> His humanity is seen in his remark:
>
> 'Go get him surgeons.'

* Subtitles

> **EXAMPLE**
>
> *Hamlet's BlackBerry: A Practical Philosophy for Building a Good Life in the Digital Age*

SEMI-COLONS

Semi-colons are often used to separate larger items in a complicated list:

> **EXAMPLE**
>
> He didn't have time for this: his manuscript was late for his publisher; Celia, his wife, was in hospital, facing a major operation; his bank manager was ringing up regularly suggesting an urgent meeting was required before any more funds could be released.

They can be used to indicate the midway point in an elegantly balanced sentence:

> **EXAMPLE**
>
> Alive, she was a liability; dead, she was an asset.
>
> To err is human; to forgive divine. (Alexander Pope)

Semi-colons can also be used (as you'll hopefully remember) to suggest an interconnection between independent statements which could possibly be presented as two separate sentences:

> **EXAMPLE**
>
> They spent a fortune on the house; it was meant to show off their wealth.

ELLIPSIS

Ellipsis is the technical name for those three dots ... that you often see used in text.

If an ellipsis is used in mid-sentence, it usually indicates hesitation or indecision:

> **EXAMPLE**
>
> 'She is ... well, I mean to say ... she's not ... she's not really from here,' Will stammered.

If it's used in a piece of dialogue, ellipsis can indicate an interruption:

> **EXAMPLE**
>
> 'It was with this in mind that I ...' Taylor was cut short by a rap at the door.

If it's used at the end of a sentence, an ellipsis can also be used to create suspense or drama:

> **EXAMPLE**
>
> There was a curious creak and the door opened ...

Ellipsis is a useful way to add a dramatic note to your sentences and can be helpful in adding variety to your mix of sentence types.

DASHES AND BRACKETS

When these are used in pairs on either side of a phrase, they are said to be creating a phrase **in parenthesis**. These phrases in parenthesis are there to provide additional information which, while interesting, is not essential to the meaning of the sentence.

EXAMPLE

They lived in a village called Limeuil – a name that often defeated English tongues – which was a lengthy drive from Perigueux.

Remove the phrases in parenthesis and the sentence still makes sense.

Note that you could also substitute brackets for dashes here.

ACTIVITY

PRELIMINARY GROUP ACTIVITY

How much do you think you've learned about the importance of punctuation so far? Try this activity to find out.

Look at the paired sentences below.

Discuss and explain how punctuation has totally altered the sense of one sentence in each pair.

1. It's time to eat dad.	It's time to eat, dad.
2. A woman without her man is nothing.	A woman: without her, man is nothing.
3. Mary Queen of Scots prayed serenely an hour after her head was cut off.	Mary Queen of Scots prayed serenely; an hour after, her head was cut off.
4. We buy stuff and cook the chickens.	We buy, stuff and cook the chickens.
5. Find enjoyment in cooking your family and pets.	Find enjoyment in cooking, your family and pets.

THINGS TO DO AND THINK ABOUT

Learning about punctuation is one thing, but you need to put this knowledge into practice if you're going to be able to use punctuation effectively in your own writing. The following section has a number of activities that will give you a chance to do this.

USING PUNCTUATION

DON'T FORGET

If you are not sure of an answer, check back to the notes on each item earlier in this chapter.

ACTIVITY 1

INSERT FULL STOPS AND COMMAS

Here are a number of statements that need commas and full stops to help the reader understand the writer's intentions. Write them out in full, placing commas and full stops where you consider them to be necessary.

1. Don't get me started on Tim he's lazy thoughtless and uses people admittedly his parents both doctors with Oxfam have left him to his own devices for most of his life

2. Having completed his university degree Liam was looking around for a new job one that offered him a chance to travel to make some money and enjoy life he had after all had a pretty grim time so far

3. Given their lack of experience in house-painting gardening and plumbing I wondered if they would be up to the job of converting not say reconstructing the old barn time alone would tell

4. 'Well Missy is this the best you can do? I've waited hours for you to finish there's a definite limit to my patience you know'

5. Turn left at the Wellington statue go straight on until the traffic lights provided the traffic is not too bad try to turn right into Eton Crescent where all things being equal I'll be waiting with Ken

6. Bored to tears by the play Susie not the most patient of people at the best of times decided that she would leave at the first interval

7. J.C. Bach son of the great J.S. Bach spent a fair amount of his creative life in London where adored by the British public he enjoyed great financial artistic and social success

8. Seeing there was no way out of the barbecue Sinead and Amy daughters of our hosts decided that the time had come to liven things up well that was how they saw it

9. As you can see it will take a few days weeks even to sort out this mess Darren is really the limit he lives in a total shambles

10. She wondered if they would arrive in time for the meal which modest though it was she had spent hours preparing cooking she decided was not her strong point

ACTIVITY 2

PUT THE FULL STOPS AND COMMAS BACK

Now try putting the punctuation back into this extract from Jan Morris's travel book, *Trieste and the Meaning of Nowhere*.

> The most appealing aspect of the Austro-Hungarian Empire at least in retrospect was its European cosmopolitanism it had few black brown or yellow subjects but it contained within itself half the peoples of Europe it was multi-ethnic multi-lingual multi-faith bound together only whether willingly or unwillingly by the imperial discipline it was closer to the European community of the twenty-first century than to the British Empire of the nineteenth and possesses still at least for romantics like me a fragrant sense of might-have-been

ACTIVITY 3

INSERT QUESTION MARKS, EXCLAMATION MARKS, APOSTROPHES, COLONS AND SEMI-COLONS

Here, the statements require question marks, exclamation marks, apostrophes, colons and semi-colons (as well as commas and full-stops) to help the reader understand the writer's intentions. Write them out in full, placing commas and full stops where you consider them to be necessary.

1. How had she got herself into this mess who could she turn to now that Pierres friendly presence had disappeared her situation was grim she knew no one in Vallauris and her money had mostly gone

2. 'Dont you dare apologise you think youre so clever don't you you have taken advantage of your friends generosity every single one of them get out'

contd

ACTIVITY 3 CONT.

3. The night had come down the streets were deserted the pavements glistened under the rain and in the dark sky the moon was making a timid appearance

4. He looked round the room and they were all there Pam with her eager-beaver eyes locked on Johns Michael looking bored as he slouched in the rooms only comfortable chair Penny bless her absorbed totally in the meals preparation

5. It was Cheryl who saw her first a wet bedraggled figure who it appeared was only being held up by the lamp-posts good-will I wondered if she had eaten at all that day

6. Looking at all the sketches signatures I could see they were all by one hand the name however I could not quite make out

7. If shes looking for her moneys worth she has certainly chosen the right place jeans tops and shoes are all marked at half price

8. Whats the matter youre not hurt are you for heavens sake Leslie say something why don't you answer me

9. Mary the twins mother has been a member of the yoga clubs management committee for several years now no one quite knows why she takes her childrens interests so much to heart

10. I couldn't understand why the womens outing had been set for New Years Eve it wasnt really an ideal evening for anyone surely the ladies husbands would have something to say about this

ACTIVITY 4

ADD THE MISSING QUOTATION MARKS

Here, you will need to add quotation marks (and any other missing punctuation) to the statements so that the reader can understand the writer's intentions. Write the statements out in full, placing commas and full-stops where you consider them to be necessary.

1. Look Sarah its high time you made a decision fumed her mother

2. According to her press agent she was too exhausted to perform some exhaustion we saw her in the club later that night

ACTIVITY 4 CONT.

3. Strictly Come Dancing and The X-Factor are forever fighting it out to gain top place in Saturday night audience ratings

4. Are you she asked available for supper on Tuesday

5. This saviour turned out to be nothing but a crook he left with £50 in his pocket and the boiler still didn't work

6. Mother mother I am so happy whispered the girl burying her face in the lap of the faded tired-looking woman who with back turned to the shrill intrusive light was sitting in the one armchair that their dingy sitting room contained I am so happy she repeated and you must be happy too this extract is taken from The Picture of Dorian Gray by Oscar Wilde.

ACTIVITY 5

HOW MUCH HAVE YOU REMEMBERED?

Test your general knowledge of punctuation by answering the following questions:

1. A full stop is required when a word has been abbreviated or shortened. True or false?

2. A phrase in apposition requires a comma before and after it. True or false?

3. 'This is,' he said, 'My brother's wife.' Correct or incorrect?

4. A colon is only used to introduce a list. True or false?

5. Inverted commas round a word or phrase suggest the writer does not take the word or phrase at face-value. True or false?

6. Ellipsis may be used to add a touch of drama to the end of sentences. True or false?

7. A comma splice is an acceptable way to connect two independent statements. True or false?

8. A semi-colon may be used to separate longer phrases in a list. True or false?

9. 'Macbeth' is a person and Macbeth is a play. True or false?

10. Phrases in parenthesis are vital to the meaning of a sentence. True or false?

When our spelling is perfect, it's invisible. But when it's flawed, it prompts strong negative associations. – Marilyn vos Savant

PERSONAL STRATEGIES

You can put all the effort humanly possible into writing a discursive essay or short story, but if you make persistent spelling mistakes, your work will be marked down because of technical inaccuracies. Besides, accurate spelling (like correct punctuation) will help you to communicate your message clearly and that means a happy (rather than irritated) reader.

If you have any lingering problems with spelling certain words, sort them now by reading this chapter. It will help you in two distinct ways: it will suggest how to deal with your own personal spelling challenges and it will also help you to brush up on spelling rules.

WHAT WILL WORK FOR ME?

The fact that you are reading this suggests that spelling is still an issue for you. There is no one way that works for everyone. We'll suggest various ways of tackling the challenge; you select and work on the one that seems to suit your working method best. To back this up, we will offer you a guide to basic spelling rules that you might have forgotten or missed out on earlier in your education.

MAKE SUBJECT-SPECIFIC LISTS

The chances are that you are reading this chapter with an upcoming written assessment very much in mind, and you want to avoid spelling mistakes. One way to tackle this is to organise words that you find awkward into subject specific lists.

Take writing about literature, for example. You need an effective critical vocabulary to describe characters, themes, behaviour and setting effectively – 'good', 'bad' or 'brilliant' just don't cut the mustard. But more sophisticated terms often pose spelling problems! So what to do?

Rather than avoid them, try this.

First, write a page heading with, say, 'Characters'.

Now list the critical vocabulary that you could use to describe the characters (or their actions) in the novels, plays or poems which you are studying. For example, look at the list of words below that describe two characters from the novel *Face* by Benjamin Zephaniah.

Martin	adolescent, acquaintances, appearance, conceited, disfigured, gymnastics, mischievous, perceived, physically, prejudice, scarred, self-conscious
Natalie	ambitious, beautiful, callous, celebrity, commercial, disappears, independent, self-obsessed

All these are keywords in discussing these characters and most of them have some sort of spelling pitfall. So, once you have determined keywords for your discussion, go through this process:

- use a **dictionary** or **spell-check** to write down the correct version
- **memorise** the spelling of these key items of vocabulary
- **extend** your list by researching vocabulary that is connected with themes or key scenes.

You can then go on and apply this method to other subjects and topics. For example, in History you could list difficult-to-spell words that relate to the Industrial Revolution or to Women's Suffrage. Go through old essays in all your key subjects and topics and highlight and list the words that you have had problems with, or that your teachers have picked up on. Apply the 'use a dictionary, memorise and extend' process described above, and you should have much more confidence in your spelling.

LOOK, SAY, COVER, WRITE, CHECK

Memorising vocabulary is a key part of the process of becoming a confident speller. But how do you actually do this?

Many people use this method:

- **Look** carefully at the word and pay attention to its letters and shape.
- **Say** the word out loud. Listen to the individual sounds making it up: **a...dul...ter...ous**.
- **Cover** the word with your hand or piece of paper. Try to remember how it looks and sounds.
- **Write** the word out.
- **Check** what you have written. Is it correct according to the printed version? If not, repeat the process until you get it right.

TRY VAKT

With this method, you use your four senses to help you remember the word.

- **Visual** – look carefully at the word and remember its appearance.
- **Auditory** – say the word aloud to yourself, paying attention to the syllables: **hy...poc...ri...sy**.
- **Kinesthetic** – write down the word and pay attention to the shape of the letters on the page as you write – the physical action involved can help you remember the word.
- **Tactile** – use a keyboard of some kind and tap the letters out, watching the pattern of the correct spelling that you have just created.

Which sense works best for you in the memorising process? Try them all out and see which is most effective.

BEWARE SPELL-CHECKERS!

Yes – those red lines that conveniently appear under words that you have misspelt can be a godsend most of the time. But beware – while they will tell you when you have got **accommodation** or **embarrassed** wrong, they won't know whether you meant to say **but** or **bit, car** or **cat**. Only you know the context of your writing.

DON'T FORGET

Use spell-checker with caution. It can't do all the work and it's not foolproof.

THINGS TO DO AND THINK ABOUT

Try out each of the strategies in this section to find out what works best for you. You might find that a combination of strategies helps.

Remember, too, that spelling in subjects other than English will benefit greatly when you make lists of key words that pose problems for you: *circumference, contour, franchise, chiaroscuro etc.* Use a dictionary or spell check to write down the correct version. Keep checking your lists as exam time approaches.

SPELLING RULES

Knowing common spelling rules can give you useful strategies if you're not sure how to spell a word.

'IE' AND 'EI' WORDS

Rule	Example	Exception
I before E often	chief, thief, friend, believe	either, seize, counterfeit, forfeit
I before E except after C	conceited, ceiling, received, deceit	IE after C with 'shen' sounding words: sufficient, efficient, ancient
E before I when 'eh' sound	Eight, neighbour, reign, rein	

DOUBLING CONSONANTS

Rule	Example
Double the final consonant when adding **'ed'**, **'er'** or **'ing'** to single-syllable words ending in a consonant preceded by a vowel.	bar barring barred plan planned planner
Do **not** double the last letter if a single-syllable word ends in two consonants.	push pushed pusher sprint sprinted sprinter
Double the last letter when adding 'ed', 'er' or 'ing' to words of one syllable ending in 'l' or 'p'.	signal signalling signalled signaller worship worshipping worshipped worshipper
If a two-syllable word is stressed on the last syllable and ends with a vowel + consonant, double the final consonant when adding any ending	prefer preferred preferring begin beginner beginning
If a two-syllable word is **not** stressed on the last syllable and ends with a vowel + consonant, do **not** double the final consonant when adding any ending.	market marketing marketed orbit orbiting orbited enter entering entered happen happening happened

WORDS ENDING IN 'Y'

Rule	Example	Exception
If a word ends in a consonant + 'y', change the 'y' to an 'i' before you add an ending such as a plural 's' or an 'ed'.	lady ladies factory factories carry carried	If the ending itself starts with an 'i', such as 'ing', then leave the 'y' cry crying try trying carry carrying

Rule	Example	Exception
If a word ends in a vowel + 'y', simply add an 's' to make the plural.	donkey donkeys storey storeys	

WORDS ENDING IN SILENT 'E'

Rule	Example
If a word ends in a consonant + silent 'e', drop the 'e' when adding an ending beginning with a **vowel**.	shave shaving shaved come coming judge judging judged seize seizure
If a word ends in a consonant + silent 'e', keep the 'e' if the ending begins with a **consonant**.	judge judgement move movement require requirement manage management pave pavement
If a word ends in a vowel + silent 'e', drop the 'e' when adding **any ending**.	true truly argue argument **Exception:** clueless

WORDS ENDING IN 'IC'

Rule	Example
If a word ends in 'ic', add a 'k' before endings beginning with a vowel.	traffic trafficking picnic picnicked
If the word ends in 'ic', do **not** add a 'k' when adding an 'al' or 'ally' ending.	historic historical heroic heroically

BE CAUTIOUS WITH RULES

These are some of the more common spelling rules. If you're a good speller, you probably already apply most of these to your writing without thinking about it, and don't need to learn them. If spelling is a weakness, then refer back to them if you're not sure about certain categories of words.

TRY IT OUT

Try some of these activities out to find out how much you've learned.

ACTIVITY 1

PUZZLE IT OUT

Here are some crossword puzzle-type clues. The answer for each one needs to be a **correctly spelled** word. If you get stuck on the spelling, look back through this section. Work with a partner on the ones you find difficult.

contd

ACTIVITY 1 CONT.

1. You get into one of these if you fall out with your friends.

2. Doing this with drugs or people will get you into serious trouble with the law.

Hint: This has nothing to do with cars or buses.

3. It's another word for the 'start'.

4. We call people this if we feel they are extremely proud or vain.

5. These people live right next door to you.

6. If you fight like a hero, you are fighting this way.

7. This department of a company looks after the selling and advertising of goods.

8. There is one of these above your head right now.

Hint: It's what the lights are attached to.

9. It's another word for 'enough'.

10. This comes at the end of a trial in court.

ACTIVITY 2

MIND THE GAP

Fill in the gaps in the sentences below. The missing words are very useful for most essay types, but can often cause problems.

1. At the play's be ____ n ___ing, he is a well-respected general.

2. She is poor at keeping objective ju_____ments sep ____te from personal prej_____es.

3. Air power is cr _____al to success in modern warfare.

4. Pitt responded badly to what he felt were unfairly bia____ed cri_____isms.

5. His behaviour in Act 5 bears no res _____nce to his behaviour earlier.

6. The decision was taken by the chairman of the Commons' Select C_____tee.

7. For the first time, the earth was understood to be orb_____ng the sun.

8. His emb _____ment can be heard in his stuttering words during his shamefaced ap_____ance before the judge.

9. Hyperbole is the term we use to describe ex _____tion in description.

10. The army's strength was seen as some sort of gu_____tee of security.

ACTIVITY 3

DO YOUR LEVEL BEST

Key http://www.ozspeller.com/gradeadv.html into your browser. You will be presented with 27 lists of increasingly difficult words to spell. This will not only help your spelling but will develop your vocabulary, too. If you are feeling ambitious, try starting at Level 20. If this is too challenging, slip back a couple of levels until you find a level you are comfortable with.

Keep a diary of the levels you've attempted. Write down your scores, and any words that gave you trouble. Concentrate particularly on words that you think might be useful in your subjects.

ACTIVITY 4

HOW GOOD AN EDITOR ARE YOU?

Copy editing your work before you hand it into your teacher is a really useful habit to get into. It will help you to catch any misspelt words and also any silly mistakes.

Try copy editing the passage below – but only for spelling mistakes.

Nitrogen is an elemant essential to all life but nitrogen comppounds are 'extras' largely produced thorugh energy consumption. Nitrogen oxides effect the nitrogen cycle, and when high temperature oxidation and chemical conversions form nitrodgen dioxide, physical effects are possible. NO2 forms the depressing brown in smog. It irritates our eyes and blurs our envirnoment. In animal studies, NO2 has been also shone to be hte most dangerous among the eight nigrogen oxides. Inhaled, NO2 reacts quickly with lung issue and causes cell injury and cell death. Biochemical experiments indicate that the region of the lung most reponsible for respiration, the region bounded by the terminal respiratory bronchioles and the alveoli, is most affected by inhaled NO2. Lung injury seems related more to the concentration of NO2 than to the lenhgt of exposure, but even small concentations for less then a hour have caused breatheing difficulties for some people.

THINGS TO DO AND THINK ABOUT

Get into the habit of editing all your work for spelling, punctuation and just general grammatical sense. It's a useful skill, both for now and in the future, and it might save you a few red faces.

I keep going over a sentence. I nag it, gnaw it, pat and flatter it.

– Janet Flanner

SIMPLE AND COMPOUND SENTENCES

Well-structured essays rely on well-structured paragraphs. And well-structured paragraphs rely on carefully crafted sentences. Why? Because if you are faced with a series of long, boring sentences you'll probably give up and stop reading. Even the most gripping content falls flat if the sentences plod on relentlessly. And here's the thing: even quite dull material can be made more interesting by using imaginative sentence structure.

VARYING SENTENCE STRUCTURE

To keep readers reading, you must offer them variety in sentence structure. Here's what happens when we don't:

While there is nothing technically wrong with the paragraph on the left, to be honest, it is pretty boring. Why? There are a number of reasons – all of them connected with sentence structure. After the first sentence, the other sentences begin in only two ways: *It is ...* (x2) or *They ...* + verb (x2). These sentences are also roughly of the same medium length.

Underneath is the same piece of information with the same topic sentences, but it has been given a little more life. Although the content isn't any more fascinating, the variation in sentence structures and sentence lengths has created a more readable paragraph.

So there can be quite a few possibilities for varying sentence structure. Let's look at some of them in more detail.

> Viral advertising refers to the rapid spreading of product awareness through the internet. It is called 'viral' because the advertising spreads very rapidly like a virus. It is passed from person to person via the internet. They do this normally when they find the advertising either very unusual, very compelling or very funny. They want their friends and associates to enjoy it, too.

| **EXAMPLE** | I like studying French in Paris. |

Simple sentence	Compound sentence	Complex sentence
I like studying French in Paris.	I like studying French in Paris, but life here is expensive.	Since I enjoy living in foreign countries, I like studying French in Paris, although life here is expensive.
Question Why do I like studying French in Paris?	**Command** Study French in Paris! Go!	**Minor sentences** So, French... Mmm...In Paris? Well, maybe!

> Viral advertising refers to the rapid spreading of product awareness through the internet. Why viral? Well, imagine how a virus spreads. From person to person. Rapidly. So, when people find internet advertising which seems really unusual, strikingly compelling or hilariously funny, they want to share their enjoyment with their friends and associates. So, via the internet, they pass it on. Just as they would a virus.

SIMPLE SENTENCES

A simple sentence has a subject, a predicate and one finite verb.

- The **subject** is who or what the sentence is about: *I*
- The **predicate** is simply the rest of the sentence which tells you something about the subject: ***studying French in Paris***
- The **finite** verb is a verb that has a subject and shows tense: *I like*. It also has to 'agree' with the subject (or in other words make sense when it's attached to the subject): So, *I like*, not *I likes*. We use simple sentences a lot to convey basic information.

- There was no salt on the table.
- We need regular treats.
- Tallinn is the elegant capital of Estonia.

In fact, they can create a powerful effect when used after a much longer sentence:

EXAMPLE

Whenever I feel down, I dream of spending afternoons in Oxford Street, strolling from shop to shop, trying on jeans in River Island, browsing in HMV, sipping coffee leisurely in Cafe Nero, enjoying, in short, the self-indulgent life of retail therapy. Therapy, however, needs money.

The leisurely, stress-free afternoon in sentence one is abruptly cut short with the reality check that comes with that short sentence immediately after it. Never underestimate the power of the short simple sentence when it is well placed after a lengthier one.

Considerations

If you use them in moderation, simple sentences are a useful tool in your writing kit; used too often they create a rather choppy, jerky paragraph, especially if your sentences are all roughly the same length. To avoid this happening, you can use the compound sentence.

COMPOUND SENTENCES

A compound sentence is made up of two or more independent statements (or clauses) that make sense on their own and that are joined by a conjunction.

The commonest conjunctions that we use in compound sentences are **but** and **and** – for example:

But	'But' introduces a contrasting, usually negative idea into your sentence:
	EXAMPLE
	I like studying French in Paris *but* life here is expensive.
And	'And' introduces a new, non-contrasting idea to an existing statement in your sentence:
	EXAMPLE
	I like studying French in Paris *and* I also love French cuisine.

There are also other conjunctions that you can use to turn simple sentences into more interesting compound ones:

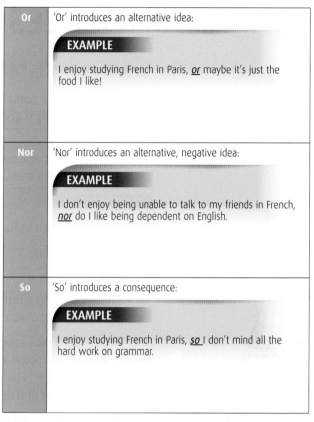

Or	'Or' introduces an alternative idea:
	EXAMPLE
	I enjoy studying French in Paris, *or* maybe it's just the food I like!
Nor	'Nor' introduces an alternative, negative idea:
	EXAMPLE
	I don't enjoy being unable to talk to my friends in French, *nor* do I like being dependent on English.
So	'So' introduces a consequence:
	EXAMPLE
	I enjoy studying French in Paris, *so* I don't mind all the hard work on grammar.

By using these **coordinating conjunctions** in compound sentences, you can get away from the choppy, jerky effect caused by too many simple sentences. But overuse them and people will get bored with your writing. The key is to vary your sentence structure, and there's a third type of sentence that will help you to do this: the complex sentence.

THINGS TO DO AND THINK ABOUT

It is easy to get into a sentence structure rut. Before handing in any draft, always check out your sentences for variety. Get into the habit of questioning your sentence structure in every paragraph.

COMPLEX SENTENCES 1

WHAT IS A SUBORDINATE CLAUSE?

A complex sentence contains a subordinate clause – sometimes more than one. A subordinate clause is given this name because it depends on the main clause to make sense.

You already know that a sentence which has one finite verb and which makes sense on its own is called a main clause.

EXAMPLES

I *like* studying French in Paris.

Life here *is* expensive.

So if you walked into a room and announced, 'I like studying French in Paris,' people would know what you were talking about.

But if you walked into a room and said, 'since I enjoy living in foreign countries,' you would probably get some strange looks, because nobody would understand what you were going on about. This is because 'since I enjoy living in foreign countries' is a **subordinate clause** and depends on a main clause to make sense.

SUBORDINATE CLAUSES IN COMPLEX SENTENCES

There are different types of subordinate clauses and they each play a different role in complex sentences. Here are some of the main ones.

Subordinate clause that gives a reason

This is a clause that explains/gives the reason for the main clause. It usually begins with 'since', 'because' or 'as':

EXAMPLE

I like studying French in Paris *since* I enjoy living in foreign countries.

Subordinate clause that gives unexpected or surprising information

Here, the clause gives additional information about the main clause that might be unexpected or surprising. It usually begins with 'although', 'though', 'even though', 'while' or 'whereas':

EXAMPLES

I like studying French in Paris, *although* life here is expensive.

I like studying French in Paris, *whereas* my brother is not so keen on the idea.

Subordinate clause that indicates purpose

This type of clause gives the intention or the purpose behind the main clause:

> **EXAMPLE**
>
> I study French in Paris *so that I can improve my job prospects.*

Subordinate clause that sets out a condition

Here, the clause sets out a condition for the possible future situation stated in the main clause:

> **EXAMPLE**
>
> I'll study French in Paris *provided I pass my exams.*

You can also use 'if', 'unless', 'provided that', 'providing' to set out the conditions for doing or not doing something:

> **EXAMPLE**
>
> I'm not going to Paris *unless I get a grant.*

Subordinate clause that tells you **when** something is performed or happens

This clause tells you when an action is performed or happens. It often begins with 'after', 'before', 'as soon as', 'when' or 'whenever':

> **EXAMPLE**
>
> I'll study French in Paris *after* I've passed my exams.

Subordinate clause that tells you **how** something is performed or happens

This clause tells you how an action is performed or happens. It often begins with 'as if', 'as though', 'like' or 'just like':

> **EXAMPLE**
>
> I now speak French *as if* I were born here.

Subordinate clause that gives us additional information

This type of subordinate clause gives us more information about the person or thing in the main clause. It usually begins with words such as 'who', 'which', 'that', 'whose' or 'whom':

> **EXAMPLES**
>
> She is an ambitious student *who has gone to study in France.*
>
> This is a book *that I can recommend.*
>
> There's the girl *whose mother teaches Art.*
>
> She is someone *whom everyone respects.*

You can also use this type of clause to interrupt the main clause:

> **EXAMPLES**
>
> The Greek island *which we liked best* was Hydra.
>
> The girl *whose mother teaches Art* is forever drawing.
>
> The prize *that he won in the draw* entitles him to ten free driving lessons.

THINGS TO DO AND THINK ABOUT

Now go through a few of your essays to evaluate your sentence structure. Do you have a good mix of simple, compound and complex sentences? Are you varying main and subordinate clauses? Apply what you have learned in this section to one or two paragraphs. Share your results with a partner. Compare the new versions with the earlier ones. Better?

COMPLEX SENTENCES 2

SUBORDINATE CLAUSES IN COMPLEX SENTENCES (CONTINUED)

Subordinate noun clause

A noun clause works in a sentence in the same way that a noun does. The main difference is that it uses more words (including a finite verb) in the description of the person, place, thing or idea. Look at these examples.

> **EXAMPLE**
>
> His future is uncertain.

Here, **future** is the noun.

> **EXAMPLE**
>
> What he wants to do in life is uncertain.

Here, **what he wants to do in life** is the subordinate noun clause, replacing **future**.

> **EXAMPLE**
>
> Your destination is of no importance to me.

Here, **destination** is the noun.

> **EXAMPLE**
>
> Where you want to go is of no importance to me.

Here, **where you want to go** is the subordinate noun clause, replacing **destination.**

Subordinate noun clauses can also appear in different ways.

> **EXAMPLE**
>
> I cannot understand her motivation.

Here, **motivation** is the noun.

> **EXAMPLE**
>
> I cannot understand why she has done this.

Here, **why she has done this** is the subordinate noun clause, replacing **motivation.**

> **EXAMPLE**
>
> They told us the experiment's outcome.

Here **outcome** is our noun.

> **EXAMPLE**
>
> They told us what the result of the experiment was.

Here **what the result of the experiment was** is the subordinate noun clause, replacing **outcome.**

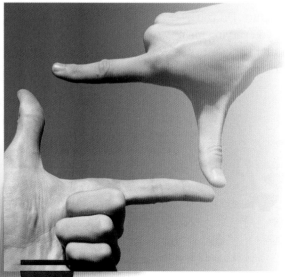

> **ACTIVITY 1**
>
> ### QUICK TEST
>
> Try this quick test to see how much you have absorbed about complex sentences.
>
> *This is a book which, when it was published, did much to dispel common myths about witchcraft, although the old superstitions lingered on wherever books were scarce.*
>
> (i) What is the main clause here?
>
> (ii) How many other clauses can you spot?
>
> (iii) Write out the subordinate clauses you have found and describe what each one does.

USES OF COMPLEX SENTENCES

Complex sentences are really useful in that they add endless variety, colour and shades of meaning to a paragraph. Just glance back at the examples in this section and you will see the many ways that they qualify an independent main clause.

A complex sentence structure is particularly useful when you are writing complicated descriptions in discursive and report writing because you can use subordinate clauses to prioritise and sequence information efficiently. If you subordinate certain statements to others, it will also help you to present your ideas in an authoritative way. You have already seen this in the 'quick test' on page 24.

Lengthy, complex sentences are also useful for setting up an atmospheric mood in creative writing:

> Whenever the moon is full, whenever the nights are clear, you can hear and see the owls as they hoot mournfully on the trees that line the road to that house which people do not visit after dark, unless of course they go in company, but even then they are wary about approaching the place which locals call, yes, 'Hanged Man's Hollow'.

You find yourself being drawn relentlessly down that scary road by this complex sentence structure, although too many complex sentences would begin to get boring. This type of sentence would benefit from being followed by a short, sharp simple sentence.

Reflective writing can also benefit from sensible and selective use of complex sentence structure:

> Why is it that when we Brits go abroad we feel that if we speak loudly and slowly we will make ourselves understood, when, in reality, we are only making ourselves look daft to people who probably have already mastered two or three foreign languages?

You could use this type of complex sentence to introduce the topic of your reflective piece. But remember to follow it up with some short, snappy support sentences/examples/anecdotes to back up the various claims being made here: *Take my brother Pete in Italy last year.*

DON'T FORGET

Remember that a clause – whether independent (main) or subordinate – always needs a subject – for example:
I ... Trevor ... My conscience ... Hunger ...
and a finite verb –
for example:
I **love** ... Trevor **dislikes** ... my conscience **is** troubling me ... hunger **gnaws** ...

THINGS TO DO AND THINK ABOUT

Things to keep in mind when using complex sentences

Used in moderation, complex sentences are appropriate and useful vehicles for conveying a body of complicated information in a single sentence. Used carefully – and accurately punctuated – a complex sentence can give an attractive fluency and authority to your ideas. Complex sentences also avoid the stop/start choppiness of simple sentences. They also avoid the potentially wearisome *and/but* structure of compound sentences.

Be careful, however, not to pile one complex sentence on top of another, nor to allow them to go on too long. Consider your reader: too many complex sentences in a single paragraph risk reader fatigue. A loss of concentration may result. Use them as a component in a paragraph offering a variety of sentence types.

QUESTIONS, COMMANDS AND MINOR SENTENCES

Although these are short, they can punctuate a longer stretch of writing into life, in a way that seizes the reader's attention or brings the writer and reader closer together. They are particularly useful after longer sentences, but they also have other uses.

QUESTIONS

Uses

A question often forms a good 'hook' to capture the reader's attention at the start of various essay types.

> **EXAMPLES**
>
> When was it exactly that I first began to notice Miriam? (Prose fiction)
>
> Why do clichés in essays annoy teachers so much? (Reflective)
>
> How can I say when my interest in playing the bagpipes started? (Personal)
>
> What would you say to a source of fuel that was cheap, clean and readily available? (Persuasive)

In short-story writing, a series of questions can bring a character's bewilderment or panic to life:

> **EXAMPLE**
>
> Where should she go? Who could she trust? Why was this happening to her at all?

You can also create the impression of an insecure character by using recurring questions in their dialogue.

In persuasive writing, a rhetorical question is often a good way to pitch for the reader's agreement and approval after you have delivered some emotionally loaded information:

> **EXAMPLE**
>
> Soaring crime figures, a growing number of food banks, a failing welfare system, an increasingly lonely population of older people. Is this really the society we want?

Considerations

If you use a question or series of questions in the early sections of an essay, you can 'hook' a reader's attention. If you use a question after a series of longer sentences, you can recapture a reader's wandering attention or invite approval. But like anything else, if you overuse questions, then your reader will get bored.

COMMANDS

Uses

Commands can be very effective in certain circumstances.

The characterisation of overbearing, high-handed people in fiction dialogue can be brought to life by using commands:

> **EXAMPLE**
>
> <u>Fetch</u> me my glasses. And <u>bring</u> me the television guide while you're up. <u>Hurry.</u> <u>Move</u> it, man.

In creative or persuasive writing, commands can also be used to achieve a very different effect. As well as giving a character a bossy air, they can also suggest intimacy with the reader. Informal commands can bring reader and writer closer:

> **EXAMPLE**
>
> <u>Take</u> my brother. <u>Look</u> at what he's achieved. <u>Think</u> what he started with. <u>Imagine</u> that. And me? <u>Don't go</u> there.

An attractive chattiness can be developed with informal commands of this kind, either in dialogue or in narrative.

Considerations

Like all earlier sentence structures we've discussed, commands should be used in moderation. Used too often, they can make your text sound rather bitty and unconnected.

MINOR SENTENCES

Uses

They are called 'minor' since they often lack some of the usual features of what we expect in a fuller sentence, such as a subject and verb. Nevertheless, they make sense on their own, even when they are no more than a single word:

EXAMPLES

Now.

No way!

At once!

France?

Taxi!

Maybe.

First, a word about the exam.

These play no part in formal writing such as an argumentative essay or a report, but they contribute usefully to dialogue in fiction:

EXAMPLE

Me? A thief? Nonsense! No way! But good try!

In persuasive writing, too, the occasional minor sentence can be used to underline a key point:

EXAMPLE

Standards, the press claim, are falling steadily year on year. No change there then.

Considerations

The chatty, conversational nature of minor sentences in genres such as fiction and persuasive writing can add colour and interest to dialogue and narrative. But if you overuse them, the overall texture of the writing can become bitty and fragmented. Minor sentences add spice to writing – but use sparingly.

THINGS TO DO AND THINK ABOUT

The importance of using varied sentences

You have now had an in-depth look at simple, compound, complex and minor sentences, and at the useful role that questions, commands and participles can play. As a result, you have an extensive tool box at your disposal for creating reader-appealing sentences. What you choose, of course, depends on the genre in which you are writing, but by varying sentence types and sentence lengths, you will be more likely to keep your reader reading. When you have completed a paragraph, go back and check that you have explored the various possibilities to the full.

HOW PARTICIPLES CAN HELP

We have already looked at how you can use a variety of conjunctions to join the clauses in compound and complex sentences, but you can also use participles to add variety to your sentences.

Participles are formed from the base form of verbs. There are two basic types: present and past.

The **present** participle ends in '**ing**'.

The **past** participle ends in '**-ed**'.

The past participle is frequently used with the verbs 'having' or 'being' to join clauses.

Base form of verb	Present participle	Past participle	Past participle +have/be
call	calling	called	having called, being called

Look at these two statements:

He called early. He found Celia at home.

To join them smoothly we could use one of the conjunctions we looked at in the section about subordinate clauses:

<u>Since</u> *he called early, he found Celia at home.*

But we can also use participles to join these two statements:

Calling early, he found Celia at home.

Having called early, he found Celia at home.

DON'T FORGET

Think about using participles/participial clauses as another way to join statements and vary your sentence structure. Never undervalue their usefulness – they can have a quietly sophisticated ring.

USING SENTENCE TYPES

HOW MUCH HAVE YOU LEARNED?

Try these activities to check what you have learned.

ACTIVITY 1

NAME THAT SENTENCE

Name the type of sentence you see in the following examples:

1. Oleg is the name of a famous meerkat.

2. I enjoy sport and seem to be good at it.

3. I'm not going unless you go, too.

4. First, a word from our most generous sponsor.

5. They can stay with Jill or they can go to a hotel.

6. If we don't go, they will feel insulted.

7. Clearly, a stupid mistake on their part.

8. Since there is no hope, let us kiss and part.

9. While I like most animals, I find pugs weird.

10. What's the good of complaining to a man like this?

ACTIVITY 2

CREATE COMPOUND AND COMPLEX SENTENCES

Turn the following main clauses into (a) a compound sentence and then (b) a complex sentence

1. He supports Arsenal ...

2. She never writes to her sister ...

3. We saw nothing of Athens ...

4. They were short of climbing equipment ...

5. He plans on going to the party ...

6. It's a waste of time taking an umbrella ...

7. Green tea is said to be a good antioxidant ...

8. Life here is expensive ...

9. Accidents often happen on this road ...

10. Go home now ...

ACTIVITY 3

CREATE MORE COMPLEX SENTENCES

Look at these groups of simple sentences. Join them in whatever way you think produces the best complex sentence. (Look back at pages 22 to 25 to remind yourself what your choices are.) Make slight alterations and rearrange words where appropriate.

1. The dog knew his scent would be difficult to follow in the water. He raced towards the wood. In this wood ran a fast-flowing brook.

2. Linda has been studying four hours every night. In two weeks she has an important exam. The exam will determine whether she goes to college or not.

3. The bike cost £3400. Neil did not have much money. He bought the bike.

4. The Dean Bridge was designed by Thomas Telford. It was opened in 1832. It was built largely by the initiative of Provost John Learmouth. He wished to develop his lands on the west side of the gorge.

5. The two longest rivers in France are the Loire and the Rhone. The Loire flows into the Atlantic Ocean. The Rhone flows into the Mediterranean.

6. I have to work out at the gym early in the morning. I need to leave for school around eight. My friend Jack is unemployed. He has all day to work out.

7. Sometimes it rains a lot. It is then my job to put the garden furniture in the garage. Sometimes my mother does it before me.

8. A fishing boat was heading out to sea. It saw their distress flares. It sent an urgent message to the lifeboat station.

9. The baby was five months old. She started to crawl. She did this every time she had an audience.

10. A serious accident occurred on Sunday. It happened near Longniddry. It involved the London train and a local goods train.

ACTIVITY 4

STRUCTURING A VARIED PARAGRAPH

Here are a number of opening sentences that might fit into a piece of creative or persuasive writing. Add at least three more sentences to create an interesting paragraph. Remember to vary the sentence type **and** sentence length, and **avoid** beginning each sentence the same way – for example:

The ...   It is ...   I ...   They ...

1. Facing Lucy were three doors. (Creative)

2. Why is it that some people feel the need to smoke? (Creative or Persuasive)

3. Imagine a country where the sun always shines. (Creative or Persuasive]

4. Pete is an embarrassment no matter where you take him. (Creative)

5. We always need to be wary of the promises of politicians. (Persuasive)

ACTIVITY 5

SENTENCES THAT CREATE ATMOSPHERE

The sentences below are all very similar in terms of sentence structure and length. Try rewriting them, using what you now know about different sentence structures and lengths, to create a much more atmospheric passage.

Hint: this is a paraphrased adaptation from Susan Hill's *The Woman in Black*. In the original, the opening sentence is geared to creating an effect of endless bustle and activity. Think what type of sentence might give you that ongoing effect.

It was a convivial and noisy occasion. Everyone sat at three trestle tables. The tables were covered in long white cloths. People shouted to one another in all directions about market matters. Half a dozen girls passed in and out. They bore platters of beef and pork, tureens of soup, basins of vegetables on wide trays. I did not think I knew a soul in the room. I felt somewhat out of place especially in my funeral garb. Everyone else was in tweed and corduroy. I nevertheless enjoyed myself greatly.

ACTIVITY 6

BETTER SENTENCE MANAGEMENT

In this activity, the writer is a bit too fond of lengthy sentences. Rewrite the passage, breaking it up as you think appropriate.

Our latest publication project involves a study of the novel which will look at its origins, its evolution through the centuries and some modern day treatments of it and we shall also examine whether the scope envisaged is too broad and whether it can be completed in 25000 words and how the project should be handled if it is felt that our time would be better spent on a more focused approach.

THINGS TO DO AND THINK ABOUT

Once you've completed the activities in this section you can check your answers at the back of the book – see pages 94 to 97.

> *The paragraph is essentially a unit of thought, not of length ...*
>
> – H. W. Fowler

DISCURSIVE PARAGRAPHS

A good paragraph is trickier to define than a good sentence. As you know, there are some basic guidelines to ensure that a sentence makes both good sense and a good impression on the reader. With a paragraph, things are more vague.

As Fowler suggests above, it is not really a question of length – although either very long or very short, bitty paragraphs will probably put the reader off. So let's have a look at what paragraphs are used for and how to put together a successful discursive paragraph.

THE PURPOSE OF PARAGRAPHS

A paragraph exists to give shape to one particular idea or aspect under discussion. When this has been achieved, the writer moves on to the next paragraph. In a successful text, the paragraphs progress in a logical and coherent pattern. This progress – from sentence to sentence and from paragraph to paragraph – is often aided by a series of linking words which we'll be looking at later. The sentences that make up the paragraph should be varied in type and length to keep the reader engaged. (To remind yourself about sentence types refer to pages 20 to 25.)

A paragraph is also a manageable chunk of text for both the eye and the brain. (Can you imagine how you would feel if you were faced with endless pages of unbroken text?)

POSSIBLE STRUCTURE FOR A BODY PARAGRAPH IN A DISCURSIVE ESSAY

Keeping this information in mind, you are now going to look at how you can manage a body paragraph in discursive writing.

The example on page 31 is from a persuasive essay where the student is arguing to shorten university courses to two years by creating longer terms. In this paragraph the student is considering the situation of mature students with families. In his concluding sentence he is preparing the transition to a paragraph that will discuss how longer individual terms will make better use of university premises.

While the paragraph here is taken from a persuasive essay, the same basic structure could form the basis for a body paragraph in an argumentative essay or a report, although the vocabulary and tone would have to be more neutral.

DON'T FORGET

A paragraph is a highly flexible unit whose length cannot be defined in terms of a set number of lines.

EXAMPLE

A still further advantage of shorter courses is that mature students, often a sadly neglected sector of the student body, can participate much more freely in university work. Imagine the personal and crippling financial cost of taking at least three whole years out of family life! Imagine how much more enthusiastic you would be about it if you knew you could cut that by a third! Commenting recently to BBC News on the promising uptake of mature students in these shorter courses, Director for Academic Development at Stafford University, Dr Steve Wyn Williams pointed out:

'Mature students want focused, cost-effective courses that do not require them to take three or more years out of a career. Many of our students who opt to do the fast-tracks are mature students who are looking for career change. They are often quite used to working during the summer period when they were in employment.'

So, not only do students benefit greatly by saving time and money, the nation's economy benefits enormously, too. Mature students who previously would never have ventured into a lengthy three-year stint in academia are clearly seeing the advantages of these time-conscious courses. In so doing, they are not only empowering themselves but enriching the country with additional skills and vital expertise to allow Britain to compete in the growing global economy. Who could quibble with that? But if mature students and the nation's economy derive substantial benefits from the shortening of university courses, so, too, do the universities themselves since longer terms allow them to make fuller use of their buildings and so reduce running costs.

A sentence (s) stating the subject area of the upcoming paragraph. *This is sometimes referred to as a 'topic sentence', although sometimes you might want to use more than one sentence (as here) to convey the issue more accurately.*

Presentation in subsequent sentences of evidence/quotations/examples/anecdotes *which will support the main point of your introductory/topic sentence(s). Make sure you make it clear who said this or where the support comes from.*

Some evaluative comments *to explain or unpack this evidence which you have supplied. This helps readers arrive at what they are to make of this evidence.*

Concluding sentence *which draws together the main idea of your paragraph and/or leads smoothly into the next paragraph.*

THINGS TO DO AND THINK ABOUT

Check out paragraphs you have written recently for essays or assignments against these points:

- A successful paragraph will focus on a single idea and fully support that idea before moving on to another idea.
- Each paragraph should flow smoothly into the next, whether joined by a transitional word or phrase or some connection between the ideas discussed.
- There is no set length for a paragraph; a variety of paragraph lengths invites reader engagement with your text.

Are your paragraphs as reader-friendly as they might be?

CRITICAL PARAGRAPHS

Next, we're going to look at structuring a paragraph in critical writing.

POSSIBLE STRUCTURE FOR A BODY PARAGRAPH IN A CRITICAL ESSAY

The structure for a body paragraph in a critical essay is similar to that for an argumentative or persuasive essay, but with some subtle differences.

Here is a body paragraph from an essay on Seamus Heaney's poem *Death of a Naturalist*. In the first part of the poem, the boy in question had revelled in the tranquil atmosphere around a local dam he visited regularly to gather frogspawn. In a later visit, his reaction to the place is very different.

EXAMPLE

At some point later, the boy re-visits the flax-dam but this time the atmosphere could not be more different. Gone is the tranquillity as he hears now the loud, angry croaking of adult frogs. His vivid imagination pictures them being there to seek revenge for his treatment of their young. With this comes a dawning realisation of guilt for his past behaviour. This is now a different world: the once gentle sounds of bluebottles and bubbles have been replaced by the frogs' 'coarse croaking', the alliteration and onomatopoeia capturing the ugliness of the din. Similarly ugly is the sound of their 'blunt heads farting' with their 'slap and plop' mimicking in onomatopoeia the squelching sound of frogs hopping about. The scene is not simply one of ugly noise, however. It is, the boy feels, one of real threat. He talks of himself now like a soldier caught up in a battle as he 'ducked through hedges' to avoid the angry frogs who had 'invaded the flax-dam'. He sees the frogs as part of some invasion force as they sit 'Poised like mud grenades', the simile catching at once their brown, rounded shape and their potential for wreaking destruction. The vocabulary of warfare emphasises the contrast Heaney has set up between the two scenes. Given the boy's earlier pleasure in the gentle, peaceful scene, the violent contrast here is all the more marked. Given the effect the terror of the 'invasion' to his imaginative young mind, it is no surprise that he 'sickened, turned and ran', not simply from a countryside scene but from a state of childhood innocence. We, as readers, through Heaney's skilful use of the various poetic techniques we have seen at work, feel something of the boy's fear and pain.

Statements outlining the subject area of the upcoming paragraph. *In a critical essay, a single 'topic sentence' will probably not be sufficient to give both the context of the episode and convey the writer's understanding of the episode's significance. Several sentences laying out the area for discussion will probably be required.*

Presentation in subsequent sentences of evidence/quotations *which will support the main point of the introductory sentences. The evidence when writing about a poem will usually take the form of quotations; in the case of a prose work or drama, direct references to the text as well as quotations will constitute evidence.*

Some evaluative comments *to explain or unpack this evidence which you have supplied. This helps readers arrive at what they are to make of this evidence. It is also a good idea to conclude this section of the paragraph with some glance back to the wording of the question. This helps emphasise to the marker that you have not lost sight of the question.*

If you feel that the paragraph is turning out to be too long, there could be a case for breaking it up into shorter segments of text. In that case, you could treat the content as a single **section** of your essay and present it as three more brief paragraphs, as long as you make the continuity of the discussion clear to the reader. In the example above, this continuity is signalled by the phrases:

'This is now a different world ...' and 'Given the boy's earlier pleasure ...'

MAKING SMOOTH TRANSITIONS

One definition of a successful paragraph is a series of sentences that flow together to create a single idea. But the story does not stop there. If you want to develop this idea then not only your sentences but also your paragraphs need to flow seamlessly within the essay. You can use an extensive series of linking words to help you in this process.

Linking words

Linking words are particularly important in discursive and critical writing where you are attempting to construct a logical and coherent case to gain the reader's understanding and approval. These signposts within the text are a vital part of this process, both within the paragraph itself and in connecting one paragraph to the next. Here are some linking words you could use.

To reinforce an idea	To present a similar idea	To express contrast	To show progression	To show transition
Furthermore ...	Similarly ...	On the other hand, however ...	For this reason ...	Turning to ...
Moreover ...	In the same way ...	By way of contrast ...	Therefore ...	Regarding the question of ...
In addition ...	So, too	Conversely ...	As a result ...	As far as ... is concerned ...
For instance/example ...	Also ...	Whereas ...	Consequently ...	As for ...
What is more ...	Likewise ...	While ...	Accordingly ...	Now ...
In this way ...		Despite (this)/in spite of ...	Thus ...	
As a matter of fact ...		Nevertheless ...	Hence ...	

Transitional sentences

Transitional or linking sentences are another useful tool – particularly in discursive essays, critical essays and reports. You can use them at the end of a paragraph to **point back** to what has already been discussed and to **introduce** an idea that you are going to develop in the next paragraph. Here's an example:

> Having seen the financial benefits which students would derive from this new approach to shorter degree courses, we see that there are also financial advantages to be gained by universities themselves.

This extract is from a discursive essay about the financing of university education. It points back to what has already been discussed in previous paragraphs, but also looks forward to what is going to be discussed in the next paragraph. This transitional or linking sentence therefore moves the reader smoothly on from one point to the next.

You can also use the same approach in critical essays.

This extract is from a critical essay about the short story 'Loast' by Anne Donovan. The writer is responding to a question that asks how Anne Donovan creates sympathy for her protagonist (Miss O'Halloran). In this transitional sentence, the writer refers back to how socially isolated the old woman is, and signposts that they are now going to tackle how symbolism adds to the feelings of sympathy we already have for Miss O'Halloran.

DON'T FORGET

In effective writing, one paragraph flows smoothly into the next. You can use linking words to help you do this. Another technique is to pick up a word or term you used in the last sentence of the previous paragraph and use it in the first sentence of the next paragraph – for example: ... he gave his **affection** freely. This **affection**, in turn, leads to ...

> The sympathy aroused by the old lady's social isolation is further intensified by Donovan's use of symbolism.

THINGS TO DO AND THINK ABOUT

There is no one single way to create a convincing paragraph. What you have been reading about here is a summary of traditional thinking about paragraph structure. But an effective paragraph can be infinitely flexible. What is essential is that it should have a clear focus and credible evidence or support. In discursive writing, it's always helpful to comment on the significance of the evidence. You should also remember to make your sentences flow within each paragraph, and to make a smooth transition from one paragraph to the next.

CREATIVE PARAGRAPHS

SENTENCE VARIETY

Varied sentence lengths and sentence types are essential to a successful paragraph. Look back at what you learned in the chapter about sentence structure (page 20) to remind yourself of what you have available in your writer's toolbox to maximise the impact of your paragraph.

THE PARAGRAPH IN CREATIVE WRITING

The whole point about writing creatively is that you don't want to be asked to conform to any set pattern. Here, paragraphs are at the service of the storyline: people arrive, they say things, events happen, characters react. Narrative is interspersed with dialogue and description. Your reader would probably be suspicious of any formulaic approach to imaginative work.

Nevertheless, your reader also needs to be steered persuasively through the text or they will become lost or bored. Coherently structured and sequenced paragraphs – although they might not have the obvious topic sentences, support sentences or transitions of a discursive or critical essay – are some of the building blocks for a successful fictional piece. Keeping this in mind, read the following paragraph from the novel *Lanark* by Alasdair Gray.

> He awoke late in the afternoon. Slowly drawing his feet from below Janet without disturbing her he carried his clothes into the kitchen, washed at the sink, dressed, gave water and cheese to the mice in the crate and rolled up the drawings he had made the night before. On the way to the front door he glanced into the bedroom. Janet no longer lay on the bed foot and there was movement under the blankets. In the close he met Mr Drummond returning from the hotel tall, spectacled, flat-capped, raincoat open over boiler suit.

The first sentence isn't the type of topic sentence you would find in a discursive essay, but it does set out what the paragraph is going to be about: Duncan's awakening and subsequent behaviour. In the sentences that follow, we learn more about that behaviour. And the encounter with Mr Drummond in the last sentence moves us on to a transition: an upcoming conversation with this man in the boiler-suit.

Here's another example. This paragraph is from the short story 'Souls Belated' by American writer Edith Wharton. Look at how it is constructed:

> At daylight a sound in Lydia's room woke Gannett from a troubled sleep. He sat up and listened. She was moving about softly, as though fearful of disturbing him. He heard her push back one of the creaking shutters; then there was a moment's silence, which seemed to indicate that she was waiting to see if the noise had aroused him. Presently she began to move again. She had spent a sleepless night, probably, and was dressing to go down to the garden for a breath of fresh air. Gannett rose also; but some indefinable instinct made his movements as cautious as hers. He stole to the window and looked out through the slats of the shutter.

DON'T FORGET

Variety will keep your reader reading your paragraph. Keep an eye on the length and type of your sentences, and how you begin each sentence.

In this extract, Gannett waking up and listening to Lydia moving around in her room sets the agenda for the rest of the paragraph. The topic has been set out in two sentences – not just one. The sentences that follow develop the description of the listening process. Then the final sentence prepares us for a transition: what Gannett saw out of the window. Have you noticed the variety of the sentence lengths and types that Edith Wharton uses here?

Successful creative writing usually conceals obvious structure, but published writers will tell you that structure needs to be there, whatever the genre. Thoughtfully constructed and sequenced paragraphs form the basis of good writing, so be alert to this in your own creative work.

THINGS TO DO AND THINK ABOUT

Here are some of the key features of successful paragraphs. Try to apply them to your own writing.

- A paragraph exists to give shape to one particular idea or aspect under discussion.
- Well-structured paragraphs are the building blocks of a successful essay.
- A well-structured paragraph often has the following key characteristics:
  - an opening sentence that introduces the topic being explored
  - a number of subsequent sentences that support and develop this topic (in discursive writing these sentences will be unpacked to help the reader to understand the significance of the evidence supplied)
  - a concluding sentence that creates a smooth transition to the next paragraph.
- Sentences within the paragraph need to flow smoothly into each other, sometimes through linking words. These words are also useful for linking one paragraph to the next.
- Sentences within each paragraph should vary in length and type. Avoid beginning sentences with the same words each time.
- A variety of paragraph lengths looks attractive and encourages reader engagement.
- A one-sentence paragraph can be highly effective – particularly in creative writing – but be careful not to overuse this.

USING PARAGRAPH STRUCTURES 1

HOW MUCH HAVE YOU LEARNED?

Try these activities to check what you have learned so far about paragraphs.

ACTIVITY 1

FIND THE MISSING LINK

This paragraph could be improved if there were some linking words to help the transition from one sentence to the next. Check the punctuation; it can help you make the appropriate choice. Look back over this section to remind yourself of linking words and phrases.

Increasing use of the internet is being made by shoppers to purchase goods because they feel it saves them time. Some shoppers believe internet shopping will increase in popularity; (1)_____, others feel the risks involved will limit their use. Online shopping is far from being a traditional way of shopping like popping down to your nearest mall or high street; (2)_____, it is a means of shopping which provides great convenience. (3)_____ the fact that internet shopping seems alien to some still, researchers believe it will indeed become far more widespread in the coming decades. Items can be bought quickly, cheaply and effortlessly when people shop online. (4) _____, buying routine items where choice is not an issue can be achieved with the click of a mouse, (5)_____ saving the shopper a great deal of pointless travel. (6)_____ some initial resistance, the modern shopper is beginning to realise that the internet heralds the future of retailing.

ACTIVITY 2

EXPAND NOTES INTO A PARAGRAPH

Below are some notes about an item of news. Expand them into a short paragraph. Remember to vary the type and length of your sentences and to use linking words.

Messages from Ankara report catastrophic earthquake in north-western Turkey. Particularly violent in Izmit region. Town completely destroyed. Thousands of people now homeless. Death toll estimated at more than 17 000. Turkish government sending thousands of troops and transport to help. Rescue work hampered by torrential rain and floods. News has aroused world-wide sympathy. Food, water, clothing and medical supplies flown in. Offers of help already received from twelve countries.

ACTIVITY 3

LINK THE SENTENCES

Here are some notes that a student has written about Anne Donovan's second novel, *Being Emily*. Create a paragraph by linking the sentences together as you think appropriate. You can change the text to help the flow of the paragraph.

In 2008 Anne Donovan published her second novel. This was five years after the success of 'Buddha Da'. It was called 'Being Emily'. The focus here was also on a close-knit Glasgow family. This time it was not seen from the multiple perspectives of the earlier novel. It was seen from the viewpoint of a single narrator, Fiona O'Connell. We meet her as a second-year pupil at a comprehensive school. This novel takes the form of a 'bildungsroman'. In a 'bildungsroman' we watch the hero/heroine coming of age. They frequently make mistakes in the process. By the novel's end, Fiona is a married woman. She is expecting her first baby. She is installed once again in the flat in which the story begins. In the years between, Fiona and her family suffer upsets. These upsets severely test their initial solidarity. Harmony is finally restored.

TOP TIP

Don't forget that participles can be a useful way of combining sentences.

TOP TIP

There were five paragraphs in the original.

ACTIVITY 4

RESTORE THE PARAGRAPHS

Here is a brief piece about direct mail marketing. Although the sentences are varied in type and length and are smoothly connected, the original paragraphing has become lost. You can see simply by glancing down how reader-unfriendly the text is without helpful paragraphing for both the eye and the brain. Check out 'Things to Do and Think About' on page 35 – this outlines the key features of successful paragraphs and will remind you what to look out for.

A recent issue of 'Marketing' magazine quoted some interesting research. As mentioned earlier, according to the US research company Starch, consumers are exposed to 623 advertising impressions every day, of which they only remember nine favourably a day later. Yet a mailing to a file of frequent flyers was recalled by 74% of them after three months. This type of impact was confirmed by a mailing on cosmetics to another relevant audience, where 70% recalled it after three months. The list is all important. And so is the relevance of the message to the audience. Think of your dearest hobby or pastime. Now imagine a really interesting piece of news about it that was mailed to you cold – would you feel responsive? Probably. It is that type of impact you should be striving for in any mailing you do. So the most important thing in direct mailing, after making sure the letter goes to the right person, is to get them to open the envelope. Some years ago, in the United States, I wanted to run a communication with the owners of Mooney aeroplanes – private four-seater 'aerial Ferraris'. Since aircraft ownership is all recorded, coming up with a list of the 4500 people involved was easy. But how could we get them to open the envelope? Well, every Mooney owner knows who Roy LoPresti is – the man who revolutionised the design of the Mooney a few years ago, and made it fly faster and smoother than ever before. So, on the envelope we put a slanting headline 'here's the news about Mooney from Roy LoPresti.' Roy signed the letter inside. We offered, among other things, a CD brochure on the new Mooneys for $30. We sold 650 CDs – a 14% response! And three $120 000 aeroplanes were sold, directly attributable to the mailing. Direct mailing is the most measurable and testable advertising medium there is. You can try different approaches, track responses and see which works best.
(*Better Business Writing*)

USING PARAGRAPH STRUCTURES 2

ACTIVITY 5

BUILD A PARAGRAPH (1)

This is a simple paragraph building exercise. The vocabulary in the sentences will help you to spot the correct sequence.

1. This conversion to continuous irrigation has led to significantly increased agricultural production.

2. In this particular river basin, there is now year-round irrigation of the soil rather than reliance, as once, on the river's annual flood.

3. In turn, this has contributed to a substantial increase in the basin's population.

4. In Egypt, the landscape has been changing for centuries, some might say for thousands of years.

5. As a result of the growing numbers and their associated activities, the prosperity of the basin has grown steadily over the centuries.

6. Boosting the increasing wealth of the river basin still further was the project to build in 1960 the Aswan High Dam, an undertaking worthy of the pharaohs themselves.

7. The most significant of these changes have undoubtedly been those affecting the Nile River basin.

ACTIVITY 6

BUILD A PARAGRAPH (2)

Here is a body paragraph from a persuasive essay. The essay argues against fracking for oil and gas because of the dangers it might create.

This particular paragraph covers three areas: the dangers of earth tremors, pollution of water channels and escaping methane gas. The order of the topic statements, the supporting evidence and the transition to a paragraph outlining the potential dangers of fracking have all been deliberately confused.

Write out this paragraph in the order in which you think it should read. Linking words should help you to piece together a correct sequence, but look out for other internal links, such as vocabulary being used in one sentence and picked up in another. This is a good tip for improving the flow of your own future writing.

But no less a journal than *Science Today* has underlined these risks, citing mid-sized tremors in Colorado, Texas, Japan and Sumatra.
This is a cost which has gone largely ignored by profit-hungry capitalists who minimise any question of the risk of earth tremors.
It is all very well to say that fracking in our own backyard frees us from the uncertainties of international political upheavals, but what of the cost to the Earth's crust?
'If the small number of earthquakes increases, it could indicate that faults are becoming critically stressed and might soon host a larger earthquake.'
For all these reasons, it is surely high time that the world's nations came together to investigate the current damage that is being wreaked on the Earth's crust.
Imagine the disaster which contaminated water supplies could bring if the respected Myers is to be believed.
But the dangers below the ground are, worryingly, mirrored in dangers above the ground as well.
Commenting on these tremors, the paper's author, Helen Savage remarks:
So much for earth tremors, but what of a second cause for concern: the dangers to aquifers (the name given to underground channels carrying water) which drilling can bring?
Furthermore, if these drilled wells are not properly capped, harmful methane gas may escape, adding to already grave greenhouse-gas worries.
Various studies by universities, governments and industry have determined that methane leakage can amount to almost 12 per cent of natural gas produced each year.
According to Tom Myers, a Reno-based researcher, writing in *Ground Water*, chemically treated drilling fluid can migrate through thousands of feet of rock and endanger water supplies in as little as three years.

ACTIVITY 7

BEING CREATIVE WITH PARAGRAPHS (1)

Think of someone you know or admire for what they have accomplished in life. They might be famous, living or dead, or simply someone who has crossed your path in daily life. Write a paragraph describing what they have achieved, paying particular attention to the topic sentence and supporting sentences. Complete your paragraph with a commentary on the evidence you have provided in your supporting sentences. Variety of sentence types and lengths will enrich your paragraph greatly.

ACTIVITY 8

BEING CREATIVE WITH PARAGRAPHS (2)

Think about a town or city you know well and write about how desirable it would be as a place for young people to live. Try to avoid obvious adjectives in characterising your chosen location. Write a paragraph with varied sentence length and types, and pay particular attention to the topic sentence and supporting sentences. Complete the paragraph with a commentary on the evidence you have provided in your supporting sentences.

The limits of my language are the limits of my universe.

– Johann Wolfgang von Goethe

MASTERING UNFAMILIAR WORDS

Impressive writing requires a varied and lively vocabulary. Whether you are writing a creative or discursive piece, you need to be able to capture the mood, character or idea you are setting out to describe. A good vocabulary is also essential for **understanding** texts of all kinds. So in a nutshell, if you develop an extensive vocabulary, it will be useful throughout your life.

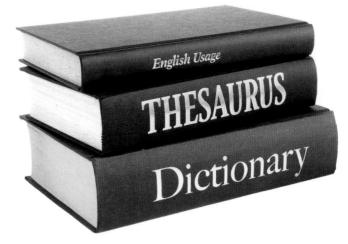

The best way to maximise your vocabulary is to read quality fiction and non-fiction regularly. But there are other ways, too. This chapter will help you to acquire a vocabulary that will prove invaluable for informing, describing, analysing, persuading, arguing and evaluating.

First, we're going to look at how you can understand 'difficult' words when you come across them. You can then learn them and use them yourself in your own writing.

ROOTS OF WORDS

'Difficult' words become less so once you get to know something about where they came from. Knowing their 'roots' can be a clue to deciphering meaning.

For instance, if you knew the Greek word for 'to write' was 'graphein' and the Greek word 'logos' was connected with 'word' or 'study', you could have a good stab at working out that 'graphology' was a study of handwriting, even though you had never seen it before.

There have been many influences on the development of English. To understand – and learn – English vocabulary, you need to start by looking at where these influences have come from.

WORD ORIGINS

Some words we use today come from Old English. Old English was not one single language, but a variety of languages that arrived with Germanic settlers between the fifth century and the seventh century. Anglo-Saxon is the term sometimes given to those people and the language they left us. Amongst these are some very basic words such as: **against, ale, fight, flesh, love, hate, read, town.**

Then the Vikings came along in the eighth and ninth centuries. They added to our word stock with many commonplace items such as: **hit, loan, rotten, rugged, skulk, slam, cake** and **window.** Together, Old English and Old Norse (the language of the Vikings) have given us many of the words that frame our everyday language, lives and emotions.

But then along came the Normans (who conquered England in 1066) with a welter of new French words. Many of these words had come into the French language through Latin, the dominant language in religious and intellectual life for many centuries. Religious and intellectual life had also borrowed quite heavily from ancient Greek. These Latin/Greek borrowings are often the words we employ for creating intellectual or abstract concepts. (There are five of these words in that last sentence alone – try to count them!)

The more difficult words you are likely to encounter usually have their origins in Latin or Greek, often via the French of the eleventh-century Normans. So knowing some of the Latin and Greek roots and prefixes will go a long way to help you make sense of unfamiliar vocabulary. It will also give you the confidence to use these types of words in your own writing.

WHY PREFIXES ARE USEFUL

A prefix is a letter or brief group of letters placed before a word which alter the word's meaning. For example, we have words such as **transport, deport, report, disport, import,** and **export,** which all rely on their different prefixes to change the meaning of the base word 'port'. You're going to look at Latin and Greek prefixes in more detail over the next two sections.

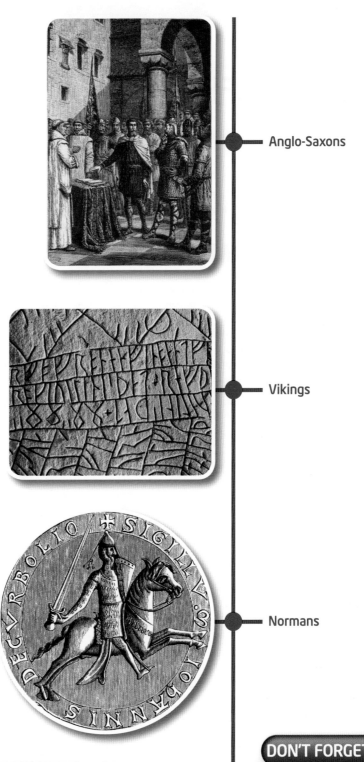

Anglo-Saxons

Vikings

Normans

THINGS TO DO AND THINK ABOUT

English has been hugely enriched by its contact with people and cultures from all round the globe. As well as enjoying a rich inheritance from the Angles, the Saxons, the Vikings and the Normans with their Latin and Greek legacies, our vocabulary has been enhanced with words from countless other languages. To discover some of the influences on our language, research the origin of these words:

cashew	hurricane	shampoo	tsunami	sabre
cauliflower	magazine	robot	vampire	amok
guru	parka	taekwondo	bog	

USING PREFIXES 1

Here are some prefixes you should know.

LATIN PREFIXES

Here are some common Latin prefixes. They will help you to work out what a new, unknown word might mean.

Latin prefixes grid

Prefix	Sense	Examples
a–/ab–	away, away from	absent, abnormal, abandon, abduct
ad–	to, towards	advance, advent, adhesive, adjacent, adjective
ante–*	before	antenatal, anteroom, antecedent, antediluvian
ambi–	both/on both/two sides	ambidextrous, ambiguous, ambivalent
bi–	two/twin	bifocals, bicycle, bisexual
circum–	around	circumnavigate, circumcise, circumference, circumspect
co–	together	co-author, co-exist, coalesce, coalition, co-operate
contra–	against	contraband, contradict, contrast, contra-indications
dis–	not, not any	disrespect, discomfort, disbelief, disrepair, disobey, disappear
e–/ex–	out, out of	export, exclusive, excommunicate
extra–	beyond the scope of	extraordinary, extraterrestrial, extramural, extrasensory
inter–	between	international, interplanetary, interval, intermediate
multi–	many	multifaceted, multipurpose, multiply, multicultural
non–	not	non-metallic, non-event, non-existent, non-invasive
pre–	before	prenatal, pre-emptive, premeditated, prelude
re–	again/back	revise, restore, restart, release
semi–	half	semi-sphere, semi-detached, semi-conscious, semi-quaver
sub–	under	submarine, substandard, subway, subsoil, suburban, subordinate
trans–	across	transport, transfer, translate, transmit, translucent, transition
ultra–	beyond, above	ultraviolet, ultrasound, ultramarine

*Watch out for **ante**– which is Latin and means 'before'. Don't confuse it with **anti-** which is Greek and means 'against' – for example: **antibiotic, anticlockwise, anticyclone, antidote**

GREEK PREFIXES

Here are some of the more familiar Greek prefixes that we use regularly in English.

Greek prefixes grid

Prefix	Sense	Examples
ana–	without, having no	anaemia, anaesthetic, anabolic, anaerobic, anaphylaxis
amphi–	both, on both sides, around	amphitheatre, amphibious
anti–	against	antibiotic, anticlockwise, anticyclone, antidote, antifreeze
cata–cat–	down, very badly	catastrophe, cataclysmic, catacomb, catalepsy
dia–di–	through, across, between	diameter, diagonal, dialect, diachronic
dys–	bad, disordered	dysfunctional, dysentery, dyslexia, dyspeptic, dystopia
endo–end–	within	endemic, endocrine, endoskeleton
hemi–	half	hemisphere,
hyper–	excessive, over	hyperactive, hyperbole, hypercritical, hyperglycaemia
hypo–	under, below normal	hypoallergenic, hypodermic, hypoglycaemia, hypothermia
meta–met–	beyond, after, across, different	metabolism, metamorphosis, metaphor, metaphysics
para–par–	beside, related to, contrary to	paramedic, parallel, paradox, Paralympics
peri–	around	perimeter, peripatetic, periphery, periscope
syn–sym–	with, together, same	synchronize, synagogue, syndicate, synonym, sympathy, symphony

Why are these important?

You probably found that while you knew some of these words, you didn't have a clue about others. In an ideal world, you could look up a dictionary to find out the meaning of the words you don't know. If you don't have one available, try to work out the meaning:

1. by working from the **sense** of the prefix …

2. … then by using what you know of other words using the same prefix …

3. … and then by examining the context in which the new word is used.

DON'T FORGET

These are only some of the more common Latin prefixes you'll come across. For a much more extensive list go to www.prefixes-suffixes.com/latin-prefixes.html

HOW MUCH HAVE YOU LEARNED?

Try the following activities – they will help you to learn and use new words and to work out the meaning of words you don't know.

ACTIVITY 1

SUBSTITUTE A WORD FROM THE LATIN PREFIXES GRID

In this activity, you have to find a substitute word from the 'Latin prefixes grid' on p42 for the word(s) in bold. Try not to use a dictionary if you don't know the meaning of a word – you won't always have a dictionary available in real life (particularly in an exam room). It's better in the long run to make an intelligent guess from your knowledge of prefixes and similar words.

1. A word which suggests that you **get round a** problem by being intelligent.

2. A word which suggests that one house is **close to** another.

3. A word which suggests someone has been attacked and **taken away**.

4. A word which suggests you are in **two minds** about someone or something.

5. A word to describe people with **many** sides to their personality.

6. A word which suggests two opinions have **come together**.

7. A word to describe the people who have **gone before** you in history.

8. A word to describe someone who works **under** your authority.

9. A word to describe a perception coming **from beyond** your normal senses.

10. A word to describe a crime which has been considered fully **before** it was committed.

ACTIVITY 2

FIND, SUBSTITUTE AND REWRITE

In this activity, use your knowledge about Latin prefixes to:

- find a substitute word from the box below for the word(s) in bold in each of the following sentences
- rewrite the sentence using that word.

coalition	ambidextrous	suburban
translucent	prelude	advent
antediluvian	circumspect	ultramarine
contraband		

1. The cocktail party acted as a kind of **opening event** to the conference itself.

2. His clothes are so **ridiculously old fashioned** they look as though they came out of the Ark!

3. The two parties formed **a temporary alliance** in order to defeat their main political rival.

4. The coastguard had been watching out for **smuggled goods** coming in on luxury yachts.

5. Since the **arrival** of spell-checks on computers, spelling has improved in general.

6. She arrived in an Elie Saab outfit of a **brilliant dark blue**. Fabulous!

7. Breaking his right wrist just before the exam was not the end of the world; he **writes equally well with both hands.**

8. He's incredibly **cautious about taking risks;** he's forever looking out for potential threats to his fortune.

9. I need some privacy, but remember the door has to **let in some light** if I'm to see what I'm doing.

10. She's such a city creature, I can't imagine her living in a flat **out of the city centre.**

THINGS TO DO AND THINK ABOUT

Try to work out the meaning of the following words in bold, using both the Latin and Greek prefixes grids to help you:

- Before the rebels could attack, the government forces launched a **pre-emptive** strike on the enemy headquarters.

- Luckily, the room's curtains were of a **diaphanous** material, giving us a useful glimpse of the study's layout.

Write down the meaning you have worked out for yourself and then try to explain how you reached this definition. Check a dictionary to see if you're right.

USING PREFIXES 2

ACTIVITY 3

SUBSTITUTE A WORD FROM THE GREEK PREFIXES GRID

In this activity, you have to find a substitute word from the 'Greek prefixes grid' on p42 for the word(s) in bold. As before, try not to use a dictionary if you don't know the meaning of a word – it's better in the long run to make an intelligent guess from your knowledge of prefixes and similar words.

1. A word to describe a creature or vehicle that can function **on both** water and land.

2. A word to describe someone who works **alongside** other medical professionals.

3. A place where Jewish people come **together** for worship.

4. A word which suggests that a statement goes **over the norms** of expression.

5. A word which suggests a teacher who **goes around** from school to school to teach.

6. A word which **means the same** as 'diligent' is 'hardworking'.

7. A word which indicates someone is suffering from a condition whereby his/her temperature has **gone below** normal to a dangerous extent.

8. A word which describes **a form of speech** which is found **across** a localised area.

9. A word which describes a condition whereby blood is **without the correct number of red blood cells.**

10. A word which describes a process whereby something undergoes **a change which makes it quite different** from its original state.

ACTIVITY 4

FIND, SUBSTITUTE AND REWRITE

In this activity, you need to use your knowledge about Greek prefixes to do the following:

- find a substitute word from the following box for the word(s) in bold in each of the following sentences

ACTIVITY 4 CONT.

- rewrite the sentence using that word.

hypodermic	endemic	dystopia	cataclysm
metabolism	diachronic	syndicate	paradox
synchronize	periscope		

1. This is an illness which is **found within** the boundaries of the Eritrean region.

2. This is a statement which at first appears to **say the contrary** of common sense.

3. We need to check that our watches **register the same** time.

4. It is a handy instrument for **looking around** you when in a submarine.

5. We need a device to introduce the serum **beneath the skin.**

6. His book on medicine is one which studies its development **through the ages.**

7. It is currently a highly **disordered and disorganised nation** in which nothing works at all.

8. They have **clubbed together to own** the racehorse jointly.

9. Atlantis was thought to have **collapsed down** into depths of the ocean in an unprecedented volcanic disaster.

10. His system is slow to **process food through** into energy.

PREFIXES THAT REVERSE MEANINGS

One of the more straightforward ways to double your vocabulary is to know exactly how to reverse the meaning of familiar words with the correct prefix. These 'not' or 'opposite of' prefixes also help you tease out the meaning of unfamiliar words. There are some of the more common ones in the next grid.

Prefixes that reverse meanings grid

Prefix	Sense	Examples
a–	not/without	atypical, asymmetrical, asphyxiate, amoral, asexual
dis–	not	discomfort, dislike, disobey, disgraceful
ig–	not	ignoble – perhaps the only one!
il–	not	illegal, illogical, illiterate, illicit: 'il–' is usually used when the following word begins with an 'l'.
im–	not	immature, immaculate, immaterial, immoral, impolite, imprecise, impractical: 'im–' is usually used when the following word begins with 'm' or 'p' and, very rarely, 'b' – for example, imbalance.
in–	not	indistinct, injustice, insubstantial, inaudible: 'in–'can be found in front of words beginning with almost any letter (apart from exceptions in this grid).
ir–	not	irregular, irreligious, irreparable, irresponsible: 'ir–' is usually used when the following word begins with an 'r'.
un–	not	unknown, unloved, unoccupied, unopened, untouched: 'un–' is perhaps the commonest prefix for reversing meaning and can be found in front of words beginning with almost any letter (apart from the exceptions in this grid).

ACTIVITY 5

APPLY YOUR KNOWLEDGE OF PREFIXES

1. 'amoral' and 'immoral' both exist in our grid. Using your knowledge of prefixes, what do you think the difference is between the two? Is there one?

2. Using your knowledge of prefixes, work out what the word 'irremediable' means.

3. Using your knowledge of prefixes, work out what the word 'amorphous' means.

4. How would you turn 'legitimate' into its opposite by using a prefix?

5. Using your knowledge of prefixes, what do you think is the opposite of 'pure'?

ACTIVITY 6

RESEARCH PREFIXES

So far, we have looked at some of the more common prefixes, but there are many more. Here are some to research on your own using a dictionary or a computer.

Prefix	Sense	Two examples
de–		
mis–		
mal–		
sur–		
fore–		

EXPLORING ROOTS FROM LATIN AND GREEK

We've already looked at some Latin and Greek prefixes, but the 'root' (or core) words that follow these prefixes can also help you to deduce meanings when you come across unfamiliar terms.

The Greeks roots grid

Greek root	Meaning	Examples
–anthrop–	human/mankind	misanthrope, philanthropist, anthropomorphic
–chron–	time	chronic, chronicle, synchronize, chronometer
–dem–	people	democracy, demagogue, endemic, pandemic
–graph	write	graphic, graph, autograph, calligraphy, graphite
–morph–	form	amorphous, metamorphosis, morph
–path–	feeling, suffering	sympathy, apathy, apathetic, psychopath
pedo–, –ped	child, children	pediatrician, pedagogue
–philo–, –phil–	love for/of	philanthropy, philosophy, bibliophile, anglophile
–phon–	sound	symphony, phonetics, telephone, quadraphonic

The Latin roots grid

Latin root	Meaning	Examples
–dict–	to say	predict, contradict, dictate
–duc–	to lead, bring, take	deduce, product, reduce, viaduct, induce, induct
–gress–	to walk	progress, transgress, regress
–ject–	to throw	project, reject, subject, inject
–pel–	to drive	compel, dispel, impel, repel
–pend–	to hang	depend, independent, pendant, pendulum
–port–	to carry	export, import, transport, report, support
–scrib–, –script–	to write	describe, description, prescribe, prescription, script, subscribe, subscription, transcribe, transcription
–tract–	to pull, drag, draw	attract, contract, detract, extract, protract, retract, tractor
–vert–	to turn	convert, divert, invert, revert

THINGS TO DO AND THINK ABOUT

Familiarising yourself with the building blocks of many English words is just one useful way to expand your vocabulary. And with an expanded vocabulary, your writing skills will be significantly enriched. Make sure that you **use** your new vocabulary – regularly – to do your ideas full justice.

OTHER WAYS TO DEVELOP VOCABULARY

Although understanding Latin and Greek prefixes and roots can really expand your vocabulary, so can building a bank of words around your chosen subjects.

OPEN A WORDBANK OF SYNONYMS

Let's look at synonyms first. These are words with the same or very similar meanings.

> **EXAMPLES**
>
> base word: **brutal**   synonym: **ruthless**
>
> base word: **compassionate**   synonym: **kindly**

So why are synonyms useful? Well, say you were writing an essay on the protagonist in *Macbeth*. You would see that 'brutal' would be a handy adjective to describe him as the play goes on. But your essay will be very repetitive if you continually refer to Macbeth as 'brutal'. You need variety. Hence the usefulness of the synonym 'ruthless'. But even that might prove limiting by the end of the play. How about 'harsh', 'savage' and 'inhuman' as well?

Macbeth's predecessor as king is Duncan, who can be described as 'compassionate' – but, again, you need synonyms to maintain freshness in your essay. So how about 'kindly', 'mild-mannered', 'gentle' or 'civilised' when you refer to him later?

HOW TO FIND SYNONYMS

Either key your chosen word into www.thesaurus.com or check out the word in a paper copy of *Roget's Thesaurus* and you will find a family of words that are closely linked to the word that interests you in whatever subject you are studying.

Note down the words that are the closest in meaning to the one you are using. Keep one synonym page in your revision file for each key character or topic. By doing this, you will build up a wide range of words that will improve the variety and clarity of your written expression – and your essays.

MAINTAINING THE BANK OF SYNONYMS

Here are some suggestions for maintaining your bank of synonyms:

- Make a list of common words required for or associated with each character, topic or issue – for example: **strike, revolution, Abigail Williams, industrial, expansion,** adjectives which **praise**, adjectives which **criticise** ...
- Underline the ones you might feel you already overuse.
- Consult your thesaurus and add to this list any synonyms that you think might prove more expressive and useful.
- Insert these new words into your written work over the course of the term.

OPEN A WORDBANK OF ANTONYMS

Antonyms are the opposite of the word on which you have focused. For example, suppose you were writing about an industry that had not kept up with the times. You might want to contrast it with other industries that had. Here are some antonyms that could prove useful:

base word: **old-fashioned**

antonyms: **modern, contemporary, current, up-to-date, in vogue**

You will find that your thesaurus – whether online or paper – will give you synonyms and antonyms next to each other. Although you might be looking for one and not the other, take note of both. You never know when you might need them.

Treat antonyms as you do synonyms. Group antonyms by character, topic or issue so you are ready to use them in essays and exams.

DON'T FORGET ➕

Synonyms = similar meanings
Antonyms = opposite meanings

ACTIVITY 7

FILL IN THE GAPS

Here's an activity to test how good you are at spotting Greek and Latin roots and prefixes. The short text below uses some of the words from the grids in this chapter. Use what you know of the meanings of prefixes and roots to fill in the gaps in the underlined words. Use the context to help you.

Robbie Czajka III, banker and ....anthropist, well-known for his em..... with the homeless, has been in ...tracted negotiations with the local authorities to allow an abandoned hostel on the ....phery of Oldtown to re.... to its original purpose. The authorities, however, seem somewhat ambi...... in their response. 'The meta......... of the dilapidated Martin Street hostel would indeed be a fine thing, but local residents have some ...conceived notion that it might ...tract from the peace of the neighbourhood. They feel com...... to forestall any action until such time as a study has been undertaken.

ACTIVITY 8

PREFIX AND ROOTS QUIZ

Test how much you know about prefixes and roots by doing the following quiz.

1. Give two prefixes meaning 'around' (one Latin, one Greek).

2. Explain the difference between 'hypo' and 'hyper'. Give two examples of words formed from each prefix.

3. Words which begin with a 'p' usually form their negative with which prefix?

4. Any word with 'port' as its root is connected with what action?

5. 'morph' in a word suggests it is connected with what?

6. Give two prefixes meaning 'together' (one Latin, one Greek).

7. Give both the Latin and Greek roots for 'to write'.

8. The root 'dem/demo' in any word is connected with what?

9. 'dys' as a prefix has what sense?

10. 'dict' as a root has what sense?

THINGS TO DO AND THINK ABOUT

When you learn a new word or phrase, use it as often as possible in your writing and conversation until you feel comfortable with it. Make it a part of your natural expression. If you don't use it, you'll lose it.

A well-developed vocabulary not only enriches your writing, but also helps you to be more articulate – and that's a useful skill to have.

One of the most valuable traits in a writer is persistence.

– Olivia Butler

SHORT STORY

TEXT TYPES: AN OVERVIEW

So far, we've been looking at the basic writing skills for creating fluent, mark-winning texts. Once you've got these basic skills under your belt, it's time to look at the bigger picture: the purposes, features and language of the different genres – or text types – that you might be asked to undertake.

Being familiar with the conventions of the more popular genres employed for assessment purposes is vital for success.

Knowing the conventions, however, is quite another, as indeed the quote above suggests. Hence the need for persistence in drafting and redrafting. That's why we'll be making suggestions and recommending activities to enrich your first and subsequent drafts, whatever genre you may find yourself working in.

You may, for instance, be targeting a creative, reflective, personal, persuasive or argumentative piece for some future folio. Or maybe your reading in class is causing you to think about how to make best use of your textual knowledge for a critical essay. All have their different genre markers. What these genre markers are will be carefully set out in the following pages.

Lets start with the short story.

Creative	Discursive
Short story	Persuasive essay
Personal essay	Argumentative essay
Reflective essay	Critical essay

These are just some of the genres your may encounter.

DON'T FORGET

When you get closer to exams, see pages 96–119 in the BrightRED National 5 English Study Guide and pages 90–113 in the BrightRED CfE Higher English Study Guide for detailed folio advice once you start folio work.

SHORT STORY

Definition: a short, imaginative narrative   **Purpose:** to entertain

Features	Style/language
<ul><li>Usually 2/3 main characters.</li><li>Often limited to one storyline/theme.</li><li>Covers a brief period of time.</li><li>Plot, characters and setting need to be sharply but economically realised.</li></ul>	<ul><li>Can be told in first or third person narrative.</li><li>May contain dialogue illustrative of personality of speakers.</li><li>Wide choice of language possible in accordance with characters and setting.</li></ul>

EXPLORING THE POSSIBLE

If you look at just some of the short stories which writers have created over the centuries, you'll find almost limitless variations in structure and style. Nevertheless, once you've read a few, you'll see that the above guidelines form a loose template for many examples of the genre.

READING FOR INSPIRATION

To write short stories well, you need to read as many as you can in the time available to you. You might already have looked at some in class. Here are six more. They not only set a high standard for what is possible in the genre but suggest highly imaginative ways of approaching the three pillars of successful short story creation: character, setting and plot.

'Pigeons at Daybreak' by Anita Desai from *Games at Twilight and Other Stories*

'The Lottery' by Shirley Jackson (available to read free online)

'Girl' by Jamaica Kincaid from *At the Bottom of the River*

'The Artist' by Patricia Highsmith from *Little Tales of Misogyny*

'The Black Cap' by Katherine Mansefield from *The Stories of Katherine Mansefield*

'I could see the smallest things' by Raymond Carver from *The Stories of Raymond Carver*

CREATING CHARACTERS

The aim here is to create characters that readers feel they truly know. That's no mean achievement given that in short stories we have only a brief amount of time to make their acquaintance. So just how do you set about creating believable characters?

PUTTING FLESH ON BONES

For some people, character creation comes very naturally. But if you struggle a bit, here are some ways of thinking about this.

Approach	What this involves	Considerations
Interpreting personality	The narrator or a character in the story 'interprets' one of the characters. This can sometimes be useful in telling us – honestly – details about a character's appearance or character. But sometimes narrators and characters are proved unreliable when we meet the person being 'interpreted'. Why the discrepancy? This account may tell us as much about the speaker as the subject of the comment.	Readers like to meet characters in action themselves. Too much interpretation may limit the characters' opportunities to come alive in their own right.
Profiling identity	Draw up identity checklists, one for each of your main characters. Try to contrast them as much as possible. Give details of their physical appearance, psychological makeup, social skills, personal history. This helps firm up in your own mind what such people might get up to. See page 50.	For some people, this might seem too premeditated. Sometimes characters develop characteristics as the story progresses. But homing in on one of these features when your story falters might be a useful way to overcome writer's block.
Showing not telling	Film directors often introduce characters with a single action. Sometimes these actions may indicate habitual behaviour – kindness, cruelty, impatience and so on – sometimes they are intriguingly out of character. So what motivated this spontaneous action – and what might it lead to?	This is perhaps one of the more reliable ways of bringing characters alive. Often it will be an action – either habitual or spontaneous – that triggers a crisis in the story line.
Speaking volumes	A character's way of talking says a great deal about personality. Try to give your characters contrasting ways of speaking and you will be well on the way to differentiating them.	Speech patterns are useful for underlining other existing contrasts in personalities.
Mixing and morphing	Take some of your own personal characteristics and mix them up with those of someone you know well so as to morph the two personalities. OR take a character you know well from a work of fiction you have studied and send him/her off into a scenario from your own experience.	This can result in highly convincing characters since the personalities which emerge are based on carefully observed data from various sources, real or fictional. It can also be a lot of fun!

THINGS TO DO AND THINK ABOUT

To keep readers reading, you need characters that incite genuine feelings such as affection, pity, exasperation or dislike. It doesn't matter what these feelings are – what is essential is that they are not just names and descriptions on the page. They need to come alive by whatever methods you choose. Often, you will find that mixing up a variety of the suggestions here will give you a character that you – and your readers – can relate to.

Start thinking about a character you might consider using in a story sometime in the future. Use a combination of the approaches above. See if you can establish a credible character in 150 words or so.

SHORT STORY: WORKING WITH CHARACTERS 1

Characters who come to life on the page need individual personalities to make them credible to readers, and this comes from detailed observation. That's what we're going to look at next.

PROFILING IDENTITY

In a short story, only a limited number of fully established characters is possible. If you have at least two sharply contrasted characters, you will often find that the contrast leads to conflict. And conflict is excellent for moving stories on. So here is a template for thinking about your contrasting pair. The headings here are only suggestions. Feel free to replace them with different headings that reflect the characters you have at the back of your mind.

		First character	Contrasting character
External	Name/nickname		
	Age		
	Appearance – give at least four adjectives		
	How does he/she feel about appearance? Proud of it? Hides weaknesses?		
Internal	Happy/unhappy by nature?		
	Is he/she clear-sighted about personality strengths and/or weaknesses?		
Social/ cultural	How are relationships with family/friends/teachers?		
	How intelligent/educated is he/she?		
	How well-adjusted to present life circumstances?		
	Musical/sporting interests?		
Landmarks	Greatest achievement to date?		
	Worst moment so far?		

How to use profiling

Your grid – whatever its headings – should contain a fair amount of detailed observation about the two characters. But you don't have to include **all** this information in your story. The aim of the profile is to allow you to close your eyes and imagine these characters as living, breathing people right in front of you. Here are some tips for how to use it:

- Dip into this information to advance your narrative – don't think you have to use it all.

- Don't shout information at the reader – for example: *Sandra loved Jessie J's first album.* Allow it to slip almost unnoticed into the narrative – for example: *Sighing, she slipped 'Who You Are' into its plastic box. He hadn't phoned. Again. Well, Jessie J, you know all about men like this, she thought.*

- If you are experiencing writer's block and are finding it hard to write anything, go to the grid. Look down the list. Is there anything there that you might refer to at this moment to get the narrative moving again? Suppose the block started when two characters meet up for the first time? How would the exchange start? If you're stuck, why not try this: *Her image seemed blurred. Damn these contacts, he muttered. Was she looking at him or not? He pretended to look unconcerned. Hi, he said, staring glassily in her vague general direction.* This reference to contact lenses might help you get started again if you had indicated to the reader earlier that the character was short-sighted and desperate to conceal the fact. (Writer's block overcome because 'she' is now obliged to say something to 'him'.)

SHOWING NOT TELLING

Certain brief actions by a character can save you many words of character explanation. It may be something habitual and simple like cracking their fingers when they get nervous. If the fingers get cracked, you are telling readers your character is suddenly ill at ease. Why, we wonder? Sometimes the habit will be habitual, sometimes it will be violently out of character, such as a glass thrown at a mirror. At these points, you are signalling in your story that you have reached moments of real crisis, important for developments in the narrative.

In *Of Mice and Men* John Steinbeck first introduces the character of Curley using the 'interpretation' approach described in our grid on p49.

> At that moment a young man came into the bunkhouse; a thin young man with a brown face, with brown eyes and a head of tightly curled hair. He wore a work glove on his left hand, and, like the boss, he wore high-heeled boots.

Then Steinbeck shifts into 'showing-but-not-telling' mode:

> His eyes passed over the new men and he stopped. He glanced coldly at George and then at Lennie. His arms gradually bent at the elbows and his hands closed into fists. He stiffened and went into a slight crouch.

We know from these movements that we are dealing with a violent, dangerous person. The physical description did not give this away, but the body movements certainly did. Just minutes into his appearance in the novel his character is established.

SPEAKING VOLUMES

The length and type of sentences that characters choose, the kind of vocabulary they use, the dialects or accents they employ to express themselves, the fluency or hesitancy with which they talk – all of these add another important strand to the development of your characters. Here, again, contrasting ways of talking will bring life to your narrative.

Think about how speech can indicate a bossy, hesitant or boring personality type. Or how it can indicate social or educational levels. How might

sentence structure/ vocabulary vary from person to person? Explore this to the full. It is a side of character portrayal that we sometimes forget.

MORPHING THROUGH MIXING

Listen to professionals talking about their work and you'll often hear them advising apprentice writers to write about what they know best. And whom do you know best but you, your family and friends? While short story writing is not autobiography,

DON'T FORGET

Contrasting characters often find themselves in conflict. And conflict is great for advancing a narrative.

there is nothing to stop you taking some of your own personal tastes, ways of talking, opinions, quirks even, and attaching them to people you have created. You can enrich that mixture by mixing in details from your friends and family. For example, say that you keep an untidy bedroom, enjoy reading Marvel comics and like going to the gym, you could add into the mixture details from a friend or family member such as an unwillingness to get up in the mornings or a weakness for buying expensive trainers. In other words, by mixing some of your own characteristics and those of someone else you know well, a new character has morphed into life.

A slightly different slant on mixing and morphing is to take a character from a novel, play or poem you have been studying in detail and then send them off into a scenario or encounter with someone you know well from real life – for example, a Hamlet-type character trying to decide on a new mobile phone in a shop where he is served by your geeky brother. Here you are mixing closely observed detail from fiction and real life to create a new reality. Try it.

THINGS TO DO AND THINK ABOUT

Devise your own identity profile for two contrasting characters. Give as much detail as you can. Then devise a conversation (300 words or so) between them so that the contrasts in personality begin to emerge. Keep this conversation on file. It might be useful for later development.

SHORT STORY: WORKING WITH CHARACTERS 2

LISTENING FOR A VOICE

Here is the start of a short story told by two different voices. Read both, then consider these points:

- Which version of the story interested you most?
- Why?

- List some of the differences in sentence structure/vocabulary you noticed.

Version 1	Version 2
Me? I'm just the dogsbody around here. And don't let them tell you any different. Them with their fancy job titles. 'Education Centre Nutrition Operative', that's me, folks. Aye, well may you laugh. I'm the dinner lady! 'Job titles give people a sense of self-worth,' says her ladyship, Tracy, the boss around here. God knows what name she gives herself these days. But don't get me started on the school's answer to Wonder Woman!	I'm a fairly lowly worker around here. I help serve the school dinners, although according to my boss, Tracy, I am an 'Education Centre Nutrition Operative'. In her opinion, job titles help give us a sense of self-worth. Tracy is not my favourite person, I have to say. She has a rather inflated idea of her own importance in the running of the school.

Both narratives give us basically the same information, but the differences in voice speak volumes. In the second version, the narrator is simply that, someone interpreting factually her situation and opinions for the reader. In the first version, however, we are drawn into the speaker's story by her confessional way of chatting to us: minor sentences, exclamations, ungrammatical constructions ('Them with their...', 'tell you any different'), informal vocabulary ('Aye,' 'God knows'), and sarcasm, at times ('her ladyship', 'school's answer to Wonder Woman'). In Version 1 we feel we really know the woman herself as well as her situation; in Version 2 we feel we simply know the woman's situation.

Choose one of the following:

Either

(a) Continue Version 1 for approximately 300 words, in which the dinner lady describes an incident in the canteen when the contrasts between her and Tracy are further developed. (Perhaps a pupil doesn't have the correct card or money turns up ...) Although the dinner lady is telling the story, see if you can get her to quote Tracy and **her** way of talking. You can switch the dinner lady into narrating the incident in Scots if you want.

or

(b) Invent Tracy herself. Let her introduce herself and **her** feelings about her employee. Pay careful attention to sentence structure/vocabulary. Try to capture her personality in the way she talks.

or

(c) Invent a character of your own whose sentence structure/vocabulary reflects their personality as they introduce themselves to the reader. You could consider a bossy person, a hesitant person, a mildly drunk person or a dreamy type. Or make up your own character. Whoever you decide on, make sure the personality comes out through your technical control of sentence structure/vocabulary. Before you start, list the characteristics of speech you might expect to discover in them. Are there any more that occur to you as you write? Read your introduction to the class. Did they get the correct personality type?

ACTIVITY 2

GIVE-AWAY ACTIONS

As people, we tend to dislike being told what to think. We like to make up our own minds about people and situations once we have observed or listened to them. The same is true in story writing. For instance, flatly telling your reader 'Stan was hungry' does not really bring Stan's situation alive in a way that means anything to us. But let's try changing that to 'Stan eyed the hot pies in the butcher's longingly, at the same time trying to ignore the strange gurgling sounds from his stomach.' Now the information becomes a real situation. People start to get interested: why is he not doing something about his hunger? Why is he in a butcher's shop? How has this situation come about?

Now try bringing emotions or a situation alive. Write a sentence or two about each of these, using action or actions to involve the reader.

The cat wanted out.	He couldn't stand her.
The lesson was not interesting.	The letter made him angry.
She was frightened.	Auntie Gladys had been drinking.

ACTIVITY 3

HOW RELIABLE IS MY NARRATOR?

In life, we tend to believe what people tell us, provided what they are saying seems fairly reasonable. We tend to react the same way to narrators in fiction. Unless, of course, something crops up to arouse our suspicions.

This can be a good way to establish the personality of not one but two characters in your story: when one character interprets another, they can tell us as much about themselves as they do about the other person.

Take a look at the description below, for example. What do we make of the speaker and the object of his description?

> Hutchy is one of my oldest friends. He and I have known each other since primary school. He's what you might call good-looking, I suppose: tall, with a swimmer's build. Never out of the gym is Hutchy, where everybody seems to know and like him. Amy seems to think he is some kind of god-figure, too, which might be going a bit far, I'd say. Runner up in Teenage Mr Forfar he may be, but compared with me, his N5 exam results were not spectacular. But for Amy, exam results seem to count for very little.

Hutchy seems to be fairly objectively established by the speaker in the first few lines. And then we note some remarks that take the focus away from Hutchy momentarily and that start us thinking about the narrator himself and his feelings towards Hutchy: *'what you _might_ call good-looking', 'everybody _seems to_ know and like him' '_Amy thinks_ he is some kind of god-figure', 'which is _going a bit far, I'd say_', 'but _compared with me ..._'*

ACTIVITY 3 CONT.

The narrator tells us that Hutchy is one of his oldest friends, but then cracks begin to appear in the description. How reliable is this narrator? There is a grudging quality to his praise of Hutchy. The narrator admires Hutchy in some ways but looks down on him intellectually and is jealous of Amy's feelings for the jock. And what if Hutchy turns out to be a really decent human being? How does that affect our view of the narrator? Here we learn as much about the narrator as we do about Hutchy – a useful device in a short story.

Now try your own skills at establishing a character who **thinks** he/she possesses one of these qualities:

- musically talented
- good at sport
- generous natured
- easy-going
- good with animals
- popular

Show through their description of another character that this is not really the case at all. This could emerge partly from the way this second person is discussed and/or perhaps from the behaviour, attitude or comments of this second person. For example, suppose your first character thinks himself musically talented, but he tells you his friends are always inventing ways of avoiding his concerts ... Your first character might put this down to the friends being either totally unmusical or jealous of his talents.

Write about 200 words.

THINGS TO DO AND THINK ABOUT

Keep your work from these three activities on file. Parts of it may come in useful for stories you develop later in your course.

SHORT STORY: SETTING THE SCENE

Think of the opening of many of the films you have enjoyed. Often these films take you to a new environment – one realised through meticulous attention to detail. The same is true of many fine short stories. People enjoy being transported out of their own world. It is your task as the writer of a short story to create this excursion out of their world and into yours. The physical location you choose to develop needs to be carefully constructed. Let's look at it in more detail.

A SENSE OF PLACE ... AND MUCH MORE

When you have a good idea for a story, it is tempting to want to get on with it. So you might make do with just some token reference to setting as you settle down to the narrative: a street, a kitchen, a classroom. But a story without a fully-developed sense of place takes place in a situational vacuum and lacks conviction. You are not really giving your readers a chance to **experience** what it is like to be in this world of yours. If it is simply in your head and not on the page, then it won't work.

But that is not the only missed opportunity. Perhaps even more important is the fact that characters can be revealed through their reaction to, or relationship with, the place where you have located them.

So setting is yet another way to establish character. Let's look at how that works.

When setting and character collide

Here is an extract from *Night Pillow* by Hugh C Rae. Matt Leishman and his family are the new tenants of a multistorey block after leaving a semi-detached council house. Matt is a tradesman with a feel for craftsmanship. He is inspecting his new home.

> The women could gitter on about central heating, nice big kitchens and the like, but it was a hell of a house when a trained carpenter couldn't find a wall solid enough to bed a towel-rail screw. Wearily, he got up and measured the width of the door with his tape. He rapped his knuckles against the door – thin ply on a frame. He knew how long a heavy chrome rail would lie into that. The bathroom was like a fridge. He tried the handle of the metal door which opened onto the fire-escape catwalk along the front of the building. The metal was like ice to the touch; that, and the stupid big window was what let in the cold. No insulation upstairs. He could have designed a better place himself in half an hour.

Here, the shoddy workmanship in this cold new environment contrasts with Matt's high standards of craftsmanship. The setting has set the scene for Matt's anger, unhappiness and alienation from the new situation in which he finds himself. His reaction says much about what he respects and what he despises. So the flat tells us as much about Matt as about the flat. From the tension set up between setting and character, we suspect that Matt's fate will be a bleak one. This collision of character and setting is rich in possibilities for short story development. Think carefully about this opportunity.

When setting reflects character

But if characters can be in conflict with their environment, they can also be portrayed in a setting that underlines their contentment with it. Should their circumstances change for the worse, the early setting emphasises their sense of loss as they enter a shattered world. Here is Cecilia Tallis as the daughter of prosperous parents at the opening of Ian McEwan's *Atonement* at home on a summer's day in 1935.

> The vase she was looking for was on an American cherry-wood table by the French windows which were slightly ajar. Their south-east aspect had permitted parallelograms of morning sunlight to advance across the powder-blue carpet. Her breathing slowed and her desire for a cigarette deepened, but she still hesitated by the door, momentarily held by the perfection of the scene – by the three faded Chesterfields grouped around the almost new Gothic fireplace in which stood a display of wintry sedge [...] by the heavy velvet curtains, loosely restrained by an orange and blue tasselled rope, framing a partial view of cloudless sky and the yellow and grey mottled terrace where camomile and feverfew grew between the paving cracks.

Terrible events later befall Cecilia and those around her, utterly destroying this magical world of her early years. By giving us a glimpse of what Cecilia once had, McEwan uses setting to help us appreciate just how much Cecilia has lost when her circumstances – and setting – change for the worse.

DON'T FORGET

When creating setting, think also of your character's relationship to it. Is he or she at home in it? Or does it anger or frustrate them? This relationship is a powerful way of adding depth to your characterisation.

THINGS TO DO AND THINK ABOUT

Think about a character and his/her setting. This could be someone who feels in conflict with his/her environment or someone who is totally at home in it. Write a paragraph in which the environment, the character and the character's reaction to it come alive for the reader. Again, keep this work. It might be a useful beginning to a later story.

SHORT STORY: GOING BEYOND PLACE

You have now seen how a well-developed sense of place can enhance your characters. But there are also other aspects to setting that you should think about:

- Setting is about more than place.
- Setting helps to advance the story.
- Setting needs to be regularly revisited.

SETTING IS ABOUT MORE THAN PLACE

Setting is obviously about place. But that is just the start. You have already seen that character can be revealed through interaction with setting. But if you wrap the setting around your characters in different ways you can enrich the context of your characters. Here are some suggestions.

Time of day	Just as words have connotations so, too, do times of day. Morning can be associated with a new beginning or fresh hope. Evening can suggest the end of things in some way. Night can be threatening. There are various possibilities to be had from working with your own associations of these times of day. One idea might be to have your story move through these times of day to underline various points in your characters' moods or situations.
Season	Again, seasons tend to carry connotations with them: spring – hope; summer – ripeness and harvest; autumn – the hint of an ending; winter – cold and the death of the year. Of course, you might want to turn these connotations completely on their head to create contrasts: for example, sadness in spring when everything else feels full of life. Think of moving your story through a season or two.
Weather	Weather is a powerful way of supporting the atmosphere you are creating around your characters. For instance, when something is starting to go wrong in a good relationship, maybe there is a rumble of distant summer thunder. What might lashing rain suggest about the emotional situation of characters? If your characters were subjected to unrelenting sun, how might this underline their feelings? And how would a harsh, cutting wind affect or reflect their mental state?
Objects	Something as simple as a vase of flowers can add greatly to your storytelling. Fresh flowers; a few petals scattered on a table top; withered blooms in a dry vase: all these can signal landmark moments in an evolving narrative. If someone is regularly visiting a patient in hospital and with each visit there is an increasing array of hospital equipment around their bed, how would that affect the emotional impact of your story? Or suppose that there was less equipment on each visit? How would that advance the story?

DON'T FORGET

Don't fall into the trap of describing a setting in your opening paragraph and then forgetting all about it. And, remember, referring back to some aspect of the setting is a great way to move your story on when you are suffering momentary writer's block. Think about matching this aspect of the scene to the mood or fortunes of the character you are portraying at that moment.

SETTING HELPS TO ADVANCE THE STORY

By introducing elements of time of day, season, weather and external objects into your narrative, you can effectively portray the characters' states of mind and/or fortunes at any given point. Night can offer opportunities for dark thoughts and darker deeds. Spring can suggest hope when the setting matches a character's mood (but remember that you could also exploit a contrast between the bright hopefulness of the world in springtime and a character's unhappiness, which would be totally at odds with this hopefulness). The worsening state of a garden can hint at the swings of fortune in the life of the people who tend it – for example, have a couple divorced? Has someone fallen gravely ill? Has there been a switch of focus in the gardener's life?

SETTING NEEDS TO BE REGULARLY REVISITED

Setting is not something to be mentioned once in the opening paragraph and then forgotten about. Keep refreshing it from time to time by reintroducing it at key moments – perhaps altered in some way – to underline the emotions/mood/situation that your characters are experiencing. Flowers wither; rain goes off; the sun goes in; changes happen. Record them.

These changes can parallel changes in characters' lives. Noting these changes in regular revisiting of the setting will add a powerful dimension to the unfolding of your narrative and the portrayal of your characters.

THINGS TO DO AND THINK ABOUT

Think about a place that you know and have negative feelings about. It might be a house where you feel unwelcome, a dangerous street or a particular classroom. Describe the setting and a character's reaction to it.

Or think about a place in which you feel good about yourself: a particular room in a house, a friend's house, a favourite shop. Describe the setting and make it clear how your character reacts to it.

Remember, this is not just about describing a place – you need to make your character's reaction to it very clear as it is being described.

SHORT STORY: WORKING WITH SETTING

ACTIVITY 1

THE FIRST DAY

Think about the start of a short story in which a character either:

- starts at a new school **or**
- begins a part-time job after school **or**
- joins an organisation or club (air cadets, chess club, etc.).

As well as describing the place itself, your narrative also needs to show your character's feelings and response to their new environment. You could usefully hint at how happy or unhappy the character is likely to feel as he/she settles into this new setting. Write up to 150 words.

ACTIVITY 2

OPENING THE WINDOW

Think about the following scenario as the start of a short story. Your character has arrived at a holiday destination late at night and throws open the windows of his/ her bedroom the next morning to discover (a) a wonderful sight or (b) a depressing view. Show the character's response to the view as well as describing the setting itself.

Here is a chance to think about a character being perfectly in harmony with his/her environment or, perhaps more interestingly, in conflict with it. (It might help if you select a scene that you are already familiar with ...) Write up to 150 words.

ACTIVITY 3

THROUGH THE KEYHOLE

At some point in your story, describe a room in which a character lives, works or sleeps. This character has not yet been introduced into the story. Describe the setting in a way which hints at the kind of character (age, personality) we are about to meet. Don't overlook key objects lying around: pictures of animals/people, a CD collection, piles of ancient newspapers and so on. Clean? Tidy? Cosy? Cold? Light? Dark? Write up to 150 words.

ACTIVITY 4

SETTING WEATHER TO WORK

Here are some lines from possible short stories. After each extract, create a sentence or two about some aspect of the weather and setting that the character might notice. Will the weather and setting match or be in conflict with the character's mood? Be sure to make a connection between mood, setting and weather of some kind. In each case write up to 100 words.

(a) How could he? she thought. Really, how could he? This was really the limit. Angrily, she ripped up Mike's letter. Dozens of pieces fluttered over the carpet as, choking on her sobs, she turned to the window.

(b) After bumping along the forestry track for about a mile, the Porsche came to a halt. They were miles from anywhere. Below them nestled a tiny loch, dwarfed by the surrounding hills. Pam couldn't believe her luck. After all these months, he had finally asked her out. He had asked her out! And here they were in this glorious place. 'Come on, girl! Let's explore,' he said, throwing open the door. 'Out you get!'

(c) It was getting on for five. Where was the surgeon? He had said he would be back with the results of the tests in five minutes. That was more than half an hour ago. Mrs Wilkinson struggled up from her chair by the window to look out at the late October afternoon.

ACTIVITY 5

SETTING THE SCENE

Here are a few suggestions for titles of stories which might begin with a strong sense of place and attention to setting. Practise writing the opening paragraph of one or more. Think carefully about which aspects of the setting you could develop later in the story.

Last Bus Home	*On Top of the World*
Checking Out	*A Place on the Podium*
That Sinking Feeling	*Baby Steps*

If you want to go on and complete the story, revisit aspects of the setting in the middle and end of the story that you have used in the opening paragraphs. Think in terms of time of day, year or season, or in terms of weather, objects or places that undergo some kind of change as the story progresses. You could use the setting in this way to reflect a character's changing fortunes or moods, or to contrast with them.

ACTIVITY 6

GOING FURTHER

Key the following into your browser:

'Evoke a sense of place' David Charles Manners

Now read the article by Judy Darley. The writer sums up much of what we have been talking about in this section and reminds us of how setting has enriched writing through the ages – from Charles Dickens to Monica Ali. Pay particular attention to what she has to say about how setting helps Tolkien conjure up what we are supposed to feel about the Shire in *The Hobbit* and the contrasting darkness of Mordor. There are many other useful pointers to creating a successful setting.

THINGS TO DO AND THINK ABOUT

Review your work here. What worked for you? What didn't? Keep your work on file and use it when you need inspiration for your short story writing.

SHORT STORY: PLANNING A PLOT AND FINDING A VOICE

Some people find devising a plot the easiest part of short story writing, while others find it the most difficult. The main thing to remember about plot in a short story is that there are limits to what can happen – there is simply no space in a thousand or so words to develop credibly the fate of three generations of a family or to portray the events befalling a cast of thousands.

The time frame of the story also needs to have reasonable limits: a day, an afternoon, a holiday, a week, a term – even a visit to the dentist. You should also limit your cast of characters to two or three people if they are to be well-drawn. If you want to have more, there must be a good reason for their presence. Short story writing is an exercise in economy: setting and character need to be quickly and briefly established. Because of these limitations, the action depicted often succeeds well when it draws on everyday rather than dramatic events. A good short story does not need violence, death or natural disasters to capture the reader's attention.

WHY DO I NEED A PLOT AT ALL?

You have just spent some time thinking about believable characters and credible settings. But if your well-rounded characters have nothing to accomplish in their well-realised setting, you'll lose your reader pretty quickly. Readers need to be kept wondering about what happens next. Plot in a short story doesn't need to be particularly complex or 'clever' – in fact, the format is simply too short for this kind of development. But plot needs to be there if your reader wants to continue turning pages.

What makes a good plot?

There are probably as many short story plots as there are short stories. Read a few from the list at the beginning of this section and you'll find that writers like to surprise their readers by their inventiveness. However, the following features are common to many short stories:

- A settled situation involving a minimum number of characters (perhaps two or three).
- A complication deriving from something happening: a letter arriving, an accident, a serious illness, a new character appearing, the loss of someone or something.
- An increase in tension due to the new situation.
- A crisis leading to a turning point in the affairs of all concerned.
- An ending with a perceived change in matters compared with how they stood at the start. Perhaps the unhappy are now happier, perhaps a relationship has altered – for the better or the worse – or perhaps characters have simply changed their view of themselves or someone else. Or perhaps the reader has changed their perception of a character or situation.

There are many excellent short stories that don't follow this outline at all, or follow only some parts of it. But it is a practical way for apprentice writers to get into prose fiction.

DON'T FORGET

The short story outline that we've discussed here is frequently the basis for a blockbuster film. Think about any you have seen recently. There is often a settled situation, which is changed abruptly by something new happening. This in turn leads to a crisis, and then to a changed situation once events have sorted themselves out. Your short story is a miniaturised version of this.

FINDING A VOICE

You have characters, setting and plot. Now you just have to tell the story. There are probably three basic methods for establishing a narrative voice, and each has its advantages and drawbacks. Let's consider them.

Narrative voice	Advantages	Drawbacks	Example
The 'first-person' narrative	By using 'I', you are inviting readers into the thought processes of the character. You are establishing a close relationship with your readers, by getting them to view events through your eyes and experience them through your senses.	This method does not allow you to keep tabs on the actions of other characters when they are not present in a scene with you. And what are **they** thinking? We can only judge by their actions and comments, but do we know what **really** lies behind their reactions?	*I rose once again to look out of the window. Where were they? Damn it! I had invited them for six and it was now nearly seven.*
The 'third-person' narrative (subjective form)	A certain character is our guide to what is happening in the story. The story is told from his/her point of view. Like the 'I' version, this leads you into the thoughts of the character and a bond can be forged between reader and character.	Again, how about other characters in this story? What are **they** thinking? Once again, we only have limited access to the full story behind events.	*Lucy rose once again to look out of the window, angry as to why they hadn't shown up yet. She felt really irritated. She had invited them for six and now it was nearly seven.*
The 'third person' narrative (objective form)	This is often called the 'I-am-a-camera' approach, with the writer observing and simply recording all that is to be seen.	We need constantly to be alert to what is going on internally with characters. We can only judge inner feelings from external signals.	*Lucy rose once again to look out of the window. Her eyes narrowed as she scanned the street outside. She sat down again, drumming her fingers impatiently on the arm of her chair. Every minute or so, her eyes darted between her watch and the mantelpiece clock.*

THINGS TO DO AND THINK ABOUT

If you're not sure which approach suits your story best, why not try all three for the opening paragraphs? Is there one that works better than another for you?

SHORT STORY: WHERE DO I BEGIN?

Once you have gathered together your thoughts on character, setting, plot and narrative stance, there is still another question to address: where do you start the story?

THREE BASIC POSSIBILITIES

	Implications
Chronological order	When in doubt about explaining something, you are often told to 'begin at the beginning'. It is also the most straightforward way of imposing a narrative structure on your story. But you need to be sure to bring your setting and characters crisply to life very quickly if you are to keep your readers on board. Overly long descriptions of either character or setting risk losing readers – hence the need to establish characters and setting with some of the time-saving techniques suggested earlier. Don't overlook these in your rush to get on with the narrative. It is a question of striking a balance between plot versus characters/setting.
Flash-forward	This is a technique popular with many film-makers. The story begins at a crisis moment in the plot, with many details and references not quite clear to readers at once – for example, a laptop is thrown violently to the ground; a phone is slammed down; an expensive bunch of flowers goes flying out of a window. But the drama and intrigue are sufficient for the reader to want to keep reading. What is essential here is that once you have created this dramatic opening, you go back in the following paragraphs to explain carefully what was not clear to begin with. A confused reader gets irritated and stops reading.
Flash-to-finish	This, too, is a fairly common device in story telling on the big screen. The story begins at the end of events – for example, people leave a party clearly unhappy; a child emerges from hospital; a couple disembark from a lifeboat. Like the flash forward technique, there will probably be many details and references that don't make much sense to the reader at this point. But if these details and references are sufficiently interesting in what they reveal about the event, the characters involved and the setting itself, the reader will be gripped and wonder about how these events came to happen. They will want to read on. Remember that you have to explain the details in your following narrative or the reader will be confused and irritated – and give up.

⚙ ACTIVITY 1

WHOSE VOICE?

Here is a scenario for a possible short story.

A boy/girl has always wanted to be a musician/sportsman. His/her parents have always wanted him/her to be a lawyer. They have always ignored any hints about his/her plans for the future. Brilliant exam results have now just been received. The boy/girl decides the moment has come to make it clear he/she will never be a lawyer. Choose one of the following:

(a) Create your own story, structured from the outline provided here.
   You will need to decide:

- who is telling the story (the boy/girl, a parent)
- which narrative stance you are choosing (first-person or third-person – subjective or objective)
- which time format you are choosing (chronological, flash-forward or flash-to-finish).

or

(b) If you are short of time, try writing an opening paragraph, a paragraph from the middle somewhere (perhaps the crisis moment?) and a concluding paragraph.

Now you have explored the story from your chosen viewpoint, use the same material to tell the same story from the viewpoint of someone else in the family.

ACTIVITY 2

A MOMENT IN TIME

Here is a crisis point in a possible short story. Try to create:

- a possible opening paragraph for it
- a possible concluding paragraph.

> 'We wouldn't want any unpleasantness now, madam, would we? If you would kindly accompany me to the store's security office...' He was being very polite, but there was no mistaking the steel lying just underneath the surface of the store detective's words. Gail felt her face redden. People were looking. My God, what had she done? What had she done? Far from helping Alec, she had messed up both their lives. It was all over. Wearily, she followed the broad back of the detective. What would Alec say? She couldn't bear it if he lost his temper again.

Take care to include details of setting and both characters in your draft wherever you place them.

DON'T FORGET +

Although activities on this page are intended to develop your skills in narrative structuring, remember the importance of establishing setting and character.

ACTIVITY 3

SO WHERE DID IT GO WRONG?

Here is a concluding paragraph where the writer has flashed forward to the very end of the story. Either:

- write the opening paragraph
- write the crisis/turning point in the story
- write the complete story.

Try to pick up all the clues to character and setting offered here as you go back to create your own story – that is, relations with father, home and cat.

> Avoiding the step that always creaked, Nick crept down the stairs, stopping every so often to check if all was still quiet in his dad's bedroom. Not a sound. Like a grey shadow, the cat brushed lightly against his jeans, hopeful as ever of something to eat, even at this ungodly hour. 'Oh, Soph, not now. Go away. Shoo. Go!' he hissed. The cat regarded him indignantly, then preceded him down the last few steps to the hallway, tail waving like a furry banner. Despite the tension of the moment, Nick had to smile. He would miss all this. Looking around for the last time at the familiar objects he had known for nearly twenty years, he slipped the rucksack onto his back. This was it. He was off.

THINGS TO DO AND THINK ABOUT

No matter how you choose to tell your story, aim to give it a shape/structure that holds it together as a unified piece of writing, not just a baggy collection of incidents. Read the first paragraph and then the last. Will readers see a connection of some kind? Sometimes this can be brought about by a noticeable change in circumstances or attitudes of key people. An image you employed at the beginning can also be subtly changed in the final paragraph. Sometimes contrasts in opening and closing settings can give your story the effect of being carefully crafted.

PERSONAL ESSAY

Definition: an account of an event, an experience, a time or incident personal to the writer

Purpose: to entertain; to share experience; to share insight

Features	Style/language
• Narrative grounded in reality. • Reveals insights gathered from events described.	• Frequent use of personal pronouns 'I' and 'we'. • Similarly rich in language exploration as short story.

WHAT DOES A PERSONAL ESSAY SHARE WITH CREATIVE WRITING?

Much of what you have learned about creative writing can be carried over into the writing of a personal essay. In a personal essay, character and setting have to come across to the reader just as enjoyably as they do in an imaginative piece. You also need to decide on the way your narrative is going to unfold: chronologically, flash-forward or a flash-to-finish. Think, too, about using metaphors, similes, onomatopoeia, alliteration and other similar devices to enrich your text, as you would do in a short story.

And – as is the case with a short story – the events described do not need to be earth-shattering. You do not need to be a medal-winning athlete or an award-winning musician or actor for your experience to be interesting. The close examination of your experience and your response to it is what will interest readers. This is, again, where your ability to recreate setting and characters will be all important.

HOW DOES A PERSONAL ESSAY DIFFER FROM A CREATIVE ESSAY?

The main difference is that your personal essay is grounded in reality – your reality – the reality of your own lived experience.

Another difference is the need to convey something of what you have taken away from this experience: it is, after all, a 'personal' essay and not simply a descriptive essay of an event, episode or experience.

Here is how travel writer Ina Caro rounds off her description of a holiday spent travelling all over France. She spent her last night going to a performance at the beautiful Paris theatre, the Opera Garnier. Note how her response to what she is seeing and experiencing

is woven into her imaginative narrative. Note, too, the prominent use of 'I'; this is very much her reaction to what she finds around her. We learn a lot about her as well as the Opera Garnier:

> The Opera Garnier is truly a palace of dreams, a colourful gem sparkling in a gray Paris. That afternoon, as we walked up the wide staircase composed of thirty-three varieties of different coloured marbles, I tried to imagine it filled with women whose nineteenth century ball gowns were so wide that they were compared to fully rigged ships. When we entered the theatre, I looked at the ceiling designed by Marc Chagall, which was definitely not nineteenth century, but somehow it worked. Seated in the centre of the theatre, I looked at the boxes on either side, which were arranged so that the audience could more easily see one another, and tried to imagine them filled with nineteenth century occupants, the men in formal black and white, the women in gowns of silk threaded with gold metallic strands and crystal beads. Our seats were fabulous and Mozart's music was sublime. Sitting there in this glorious palace built in a city filled with palaces, my mind drifted back to the soaring cathedrals, the moated fortresses and opulent castles I had visited, and I could think of no better way to end my magical journey through time.
>
> (*Paris to the Past*: Norton, 2011)

Ina Caro is discussing her experience in a prominent Parisian landmark, but you could obtain a similar effect by discussing some building, historic or otherwise, in your own home town – and your response to it.

FINDING A TOPIC

This is perhaps the most difficult part of all in writing a personal essay. You might think that your life isn't very interesting or exciting. But once you delve into it a bit, you can usually come up with some really good material for a personal essay.

The visit

We have already seen how a visit to a place can be the basis for an essay. This could be extended to any town or country you know well as the result of a holiday,

school trip or family event. The essential thing is to bring your experience alive for the reader: your mood that day; the people you went with, their reactions; how you travelled; how the weather did or did not match your mood; your reaction to what you saw; what you took away from the experience. Remember, too, that not every visit is a success. While we set out to enjoy ourselves, disappointments can happen and things can go wrong. You could also explore this aspect.

The person

When you think about your life, you will undoubtedly have come across characters who have made a lasting impression on you – for example, a relation, a friend, a neighbour or a teacher. Consider how you first came across them; what your initial reaction to them was; how the relationship developed; what you learned from them and how they have influenced you and your way of looking at the world.

The relationship

Your life is a complex network of relationships with friends and relatives. As you grow and develop, these relationships can often change. People you were once close to can become almost strangers; people you might not have immediately taken to have become close friends. What brings about these changes? Who is it that has changed: you or them? Have you been surprised by the reactions of someone you thought you knew? Bring the character and settings alive just as you would in a creative piece.

The activity

As you grow up you are exposed – willingly or unwillingly – to a variety of activities, often by parents. Piano lessons, riding lessons, scouting/girlguiding, air cadets, hang-gliding, abseiling (to name but a few) are all productive areas to explore. Whatever the activity, describe how you first made contact with it; your expectations; your first reactions; developments once begun; the impact of the activity on you. This activity might have changed your life – or it might have been something of a disaster. If the latter, you might get a humorous essay out of the experience. Again, well-realised characters and setting will be key to success.

The job

For those of you who have a part-time job out of school, your reader could be highly entertained by your experiences. Was there a particular reason for needing to make money? Was finding a job easy? How did the interview(s) go? What was your first day like? Your colleagues? Any awkward moments? What has working taught you?

Bring your place of work alive with careful attention to setting and description of your colleagues.

DON'T FORGET

Facts alone are never quite enough in a personal essay. Aim to write your reactions and responses to events as well.

THINGS TO DO AND THINK ABOUT

Although grounded in real events, your personal essay should be as rewarding to read as a work of fiction. Remember to use all the techniques you might use in a short story.

REFLECTIVE ESSAY

Definition: the exploration of a personal idea, response or emotion

Purpose: to entertain; to share insight

Features	Style/language
• Takes reader into the writer's thoughts and views. • Might examine topic from a variety of angles.	• Tone can vary from contemplative to concerned, amused or indignant. • Frequent use of personal pronouns 'I' and possibly 'we'.

WHAT'S THE DIFFERENCE BETWEEN A REFLECTIVE ESSAY AND A PERSONAL ESSAY?

While both are based on you, your life and your interaction with the world around you, the focus in a reflective essay is more on what goes on in your head than on what goes on in your life. Your life experience is important, but only so far as it sets you off thinking about some aspect of the world around you.

The idea for a reflective essay might spring from some feature of your daily life that intrigues or even irritates you. For example, why do we have so many cooking programmes on television? Why do British actors do so well in Hollywood? Why is a gym-fit body so prized?

WHAT ARE THE KEY FEATURES OF A REFLECTIVE ESSAY?

Anecdote/ observation	To get your reader interested in your reflections, you need to make clear how this topic came to your attention in the first place and why you think it is significant. This can often be triggered by an event or incident – but be careful not to let this happening dominate your essay. For example: *On a recent trip to London, I was lured into the Tate Modern by my culture-vulture sister. Wandering round these huge caverns showcasing the canvases of the great and good of modern time set me to thinking about what I really felt towards what I was looking at. Now, don't get me wrong here, I like art, but I got to wondering why it is that …* This is the writer's opening on a reflective essay about his response to abstract art. The opening paragraph needs to be a 'hook' to attract the reader's interest. Work on it as you would on the start of a short story.
Character presentation	The pronoun 'I' will be important here, since it is your reflections and reactions that take centre stage in this essay. How you present yourself needs to be as carefully considered as any character in a short story. If people are to be interested in and perhaps convinced by your reflections, you need to present yourself as someone who thinks in a balanced way and is open to the ideas and reactions of others. Your reactions to other people's views are also fruitful areas to explore within your essay. For example: *Now take my sister. She has quite the opposite view, finding Mondrian a painter who really…*
Language choices	Here, too, is another way in which your character will emerge. Remember that it is more attractive to talk **to** and not **at** the reader. Informal tone often works in this kind of essay, as though you were exchanging your thoughts with a friend. (See page 77 for the features of informal tone.) Metaphors and similes will also help enrich the texture of your views.

Process	Although you are sharing your thoughts with your reader, these cannot be presented as a loose collection of ideas: you need some kind of structure to shape your thought process. You might actually work through several moods during the course of the piece:

- The overall tone might be **confiding** as you take people into your private thoughts about modern art.
- It might become **indignant** as you consider some aspect that you find unacceptable (for example, the colossal monetary value of a certain picture).
- It might then move into **concerned** as you consider how many hospitals and schools could be built for this money.
- It might become **amused** at the pompous way some people talk about art on television.

By the end of the essay, your reflections will probably have passed through several of these moods. Make sure that you signal changes of direction clearly to ensure that your reflections have an overall structural unity.

DON'T FORGET

Make sure you choose a subject for a reflective essay that has adequate depth for thoughtful reflection. Can you view it from sufficient angles?

REFLECTION IN PRACTICE

Here are some short extracts from a reflective piece by television personality David Mitchell. He is exasperated not only by what he feels is the trivialisation of the Remembrance Day poppy but also by what he sees as social pressures to wear one. Notice how he arrives at a satisfactory structure by linking the last sentence with the opening.

Have you noticed those special sparkly poppies that some people on television have taken to wearing instead of the normal ones? I don't know when they first cropped up – it feels like about two years ago, which usually means it's roughly 10. But only this year did it start to get on my nerves.

How dare television designers adapt this token of remembrance to blend in with their trashy aesthetic? How dare they make it twinkly? The poppy is an incredibly moving symbol. This flower somehow flourished on battlefields smashed by the world's first experience of industrialised war – a war of unprecedented carnage which became almost as terrifying to the statesmen who had let it start as it was to the millions of soldiers who were killed or wounded by it.

The poppy represents the consensus that existed after the armistice – not a military or political consensus, but an emotional one that the indiscriminate bloodletting of total war was too terrible ever to be forgotten, that only in solemn remembrance can any sense be made of those millions of deaths.

However, this broad consensus is only powerful if it's genuine, and genuinely voluntary. So people were rightly outraged last week by the wrongful outrage provoked by ITV News presenter Charlene White's decision not to wear a poppy on TV. The *Mirror* generated some negative publicity for the BBC out of the fact of some viewers complaining about a lack of poppies on the Halloween-themed edition of *Strictly Come Dancing*. And Labour MP Gerry Sutcliffe wasn't too busy to criticise Google for sporting too small a poppy on its homepage, saying: 'Around Remembrance Day it is demeaning not to have something that is spectacular.'

If this development goes unchallenged, the next stage in the story of the poppy is inevitable: if people *have* to wear them to be deemed respectable, then gradually more people will start refusing as a gesture of rebellion against the establishment. The poppy will cease to be a symbol of the horror of war and of soldiers' sacrifice and it will become a political badge of the status quo.

It's wonderfully humane and moving if everyone wears a poppy – but only if they don't feel they have to, and wouldn't fear not to. Otherwise, we really might as well doll up our poppies with sequins, because they'll have stopped meaning anything at all.

(Extract from 'There's no point wearing a poppy if you just want to be popular' in *The Observer*. 17 November 2013.)

THINGS TO DO AND THINK ABOUT

You are offering readers a very personal insight into how you view an aspect of the world around you. Are you happy with the mental profile of yourself that you are offering your readers? It might be useful to get a partner to give an opinion of how you come over in the text.

WORKING ON BEING PERSONAL, BEING REFLECTIVE

Here are some activities that will prepare you to write personal and reflective essays.

ACTIVITY 1

BAD DAY, GOOD DAY

Before you begin a personal essay, explore the start of your day as a practice exercise. Make the details of your home and family come alive for the reader, but do not invent. Consider setting and characterisation of people/animals you encountered and include dialogue if you feel it would help to make the scene real and convincing.

Perhaps the day started well – perhaps it started badly. Begin with the waking up process and take it to leaving the house. Write about 200 words.

ACTIVITY 2

BRINGING EXPERIENCES TO LIFE

Here are some extracts from personal writing. Some realise a setting and/or characterisation well, some do not.

(a) Read all of them and decide which ones sound most convincing. What features contributed to their success?

(b) Analyse what you think are the mistakes in the weaker ones. What suggestions would you make to the writer on how to improve the information given here? Without altering the writer's information, re-write the extracts in a way you think would improve the reading experience.

1. *When I heard the alarm, I got up, opened the curtains and looked out. After putting on my clothes, I went downstairs and had my breakfast. It was museli which I hate. Then I took the dog out for a walk in the rain. Since it was getting on for 8.30, I thought it was time to get back so I would not be late for school again.*

2. *It's always the same: I sit down at my laptop, switch it on, go to Documents, open up my Folio*

ACTIVITY 2 CONT.

folder, right click for a new document. Obligingly, that nice white rectangle appears as if by magic. And then – nothing! I think they call it writer's block. I call it worse things than that when I am trying to work on a first draft for a folio piece.

3. *The traffic was really bad in the centre of town. We had to wait in a jam at the lights for nearly fifteen minutes. You could tell the drivers were all angry. My dad certainly was and I felt like getting out and walking to the pool instead of waiting for the jam to clear. I was really worried. My dad did not think walking was good idea and started shouting at me.*

4. *It was the music that I noticed first. Every tartan goods shop you passed had bagpipe music blaring at you aggressively. And every second shop was a tartan goods shop. So imagine the din as 'The Dashing White Sergeant' clashed with 'Kate Dalrymple' before both of them ran into a 'Highland Laddie'. I would like to say we hurried down to the Parliament building, but tourists with shorts and hairy legs kept getting in the way. And that was only the women! The Royal Mile? You can keep it as far as I'm concerned.*

5. *Before the concert began I looked around the arena. It was really huge. There were rows and rows of seats that rose up towards the floodlights. All of them seemed to be full. The floodlights were really bright. There was a lot of talking going on and people seemed to be excited. Then the lights went out and 'One Direction' came on.*

ACTIVITY 3

REFLECTING ON DAILY LIFE

Here are four ideas for reflective topics. Use them to practise before you decide on a reflective topic of your own. Or you could develop these suggestions in your own way – it's up to you.

Introduce the topic with an opening anecdote or observation then decide on the angles and attitudes you want to explore – for example, are you concerned, amused, supportive, irritated or indignant? Or perhaps you will move through several of these in the course of your piece? Think about how you present your 'I': remember that nobody likes a bigot! Remember, too, that this is a reflective piece, not an argumentative essay: you are not being asked to line up arguments on either side, merely to reflect on various aspects of the topic that strike you as interesting and worthy of further thought.

(a) Charity mornings on the High Street

(b) Jogging and joggers: why do they do it?

(c) Talent shows on television

(d) What makes a good friend?

To help you get started, here is one suggestion for the development of the first topic.

Topic introduced	Go down your High Street most Saturday mornings and you are highly likely to find that you have stumbled on a fund-raising morning for one charity or another. Last week in my home town it was.................... The week before it was.................. and I see from posters that next week it is likely to be .... They seem a .... of Saturday mornings.
Writer's personal view	Let me start by making one thing clear: I am a great admirer of charities, believing they fulfil an important role in society. I am particularly struck by the sincerity of the people who................ There they stand......................................
Reaction to topic of others and reflection aroused in writer	What strikes me even more is the way people on the High Street react to the charity collectors. It makes great viewing for people watchers like me. Some people will................ .... Others will............................ Some even goes as far as ....
Speculation on reasons for reactions of others	Why is it that .... Are they so reluctant to give because............................... ....? Or do they disagree with the principle that........................? What is humbling is that often the most generous seem to be......................
Reaction to topic of a wider public and reflection aroused in writer	But if the public seems to have mixed views on charity-giving, so, too, do governments. If governments gave more.................... surely..............................?
Comparison with and reflection on response of an even wider public	The British public, however, seems to be a generous giver. Last year in Britain, we gave......................... In other European countries the figure was............. Now, we are much given in this country to self-criticism, but.............................
Summing up of views and final reflections on the topic	Looked at from various angles, it is clear that charity-giving is something which.......................

THINGS TO DO AND THINK ABOUT

Different topics could well require different frameworks. Once you have decided on your topic, consider the framework you will use to explore it: your own ideas, ideas of friends and family, or ideas of a wider public? Consider, too, the various tones and attitudes you might use to explore the subject – it's as important here as it is in other types of writing to have variety.

PERSUASIVE ESSAY

Definition: the subjective presentation of an issue or topic

Purpose: to convince others to share writer's opinion

Features	Style/language
• Presents a wholly personal, clearly focused point of view on topic/issue. • Selective in choice of evidence to support views. • Emotionally engaged with topic.	• Emotive language. • Rhetorical features. • Persuasive techniques. • Informal in tone.

WHAT WRITING PERSUASIVELY INVOLVES

Like a reflective essay, a persuasive essay explores some aspect of your own personal 'take' on the world around you. The major difference, however, is that the persuasive essay's intention is unashamedly to get readers to end up **sharing** your own particular view of the topic in question. To achieve this, your language has to be as carefully thought through as the facts that you present – perhaps even more so.

LANGUAGE CHOICES TO BE MADE

If you want to persuade your reader, you need to be highly selective in your choice of language. You are far from being a neutral commentator on the topic: you are wholly committed to your own viewpoint and your aim is to persuade the reader to subscribe to this viewpoint, too. No mean task! So let's see what choices about language you need to think about.

Getting the reader onside

A good start is to be generous with your use of personal pronouns such as 'we' and 'you'. They immediately suggest that 'we' are on the same side to start with – 'we' are already a team:

> **EXAMPLES**
>
> We are surely alike in thinking that when we ...
> You, like me, surely feel that whenever we see ...

Bonding with the reader is further reinforced when we use informal commands frequently:

> **EXAMPLES**
>
> <u>Imagine</u> how much better our world would be if ...
> Just <u>think</u> what an improvement it would be if ...

Emotive language

Take every opportunity to work on the reader's emotions. Descriptions can be emotionally loaded rather than left simply factual:

> **EXAMPLES**
>
> 'hard-hearted bureaucrats'   vs 'bureaucrats'
> 'seriously concerned parents'   vs 'parents'
> 'gravely undernourished children' vs 'children'

The aim here is to arouse strong feelings in the reader: feelings of sympathy or support for those unjustly treated; anger or criticism for those responsible. If you cite famous or celebrity figures, you are free to attach emotive phrases to their names:

> **EXAMPLE**
>
> Charles Dickens, that great champion of the exploited underdog ...

Rhetorical questions

These are questions that the reader is not expected to answer directly: their purpose is to elicit the reader's support and agreement:

> **EXAMPLE**
>
> What are we to think of a government that treats its pensioners this way?

Not a lot, is what we are expected to concur silently. Sometimes, writers and speakers will go a bit further and answer their own questions for effect:

> **EXAMPLE**
>
> I'll tell you what we think: we think they are a mean-spirited, heartless bunch!

Used occasionally (particularly after a description packed with emotive word choice) rhetorical questions are particularly effective in stressing shared values between writer and reader. Used too often, they tend to sound rather hollow, so ration their use.

Attitude markers

After some particularly informative yet emotive reporting, attitude markers can be useful in guiding reader response to the writer's viewpoint:

EXAMPLES

Clearly, then, ... So obviously, ... Surely, ... Fortunately, ...

These are just a few. Use them to win readers over to your point of view.

DON'T FORGET

Persuasion needs to be kept up. Be careful not to slip back into simply providing information. While you need to avoid falling into an unrelieved rant, don't overlook the chance to slant your information with emotive adjectives or rhetorical devices.

Parallel structures

Recurring patterns in phrases are a memorable way to present a persuasive message:

EXAMPLE

We welcome the frankness of her efforts to ...We admire the honesty of her admission that ...We share the generosity of her spirit in ...

Here, the 'we'+ verb+ 'the'+ noun+ 'of her' + noun' formula creates a pleasing pattern that the reader can partially predict and certainly remember.

Repetition

Parallel structures use repetition for effect, but repetition does not always need to be so elaborate:

EXAMPLES

We cannot understand her attitude ... The public simply cannot believe in someone who ... Most companies cannot support certain of her initiatives which ...

Here it is merely the repetition of a single word that reaches out to us, but its very repetition can create a powerful (here, negative) effect in our response to a person or topic.

Rising rhetorical triads (or tricolons)

These are the technical terms for something you are probably already quite familiar with from watching television or reading newspapers. They are closely related to parallel structure and repetition. These statements or phrases typically appear in the final section of an article or speech, with each element gaining in power as the writer seeks to build up the text towards a ringing climax:

EXAMPLE

Let us hope that this will lead to ... Let us hope this will also lead to ... And let us hope that, above all, this will lead to a world in which ...

 THINGS TO DO AND THINK ABOUT

Think three! In persuasive writing, three is a magic number. Parallel structures and rising rhetorical triads give you a fine opportunity to exploit this. Three-part phrases stick in the memory and have a pleasing ring to them. Look back at some of the examples in this section. Keep them in mind, especially when you come to your concluding paragraph.

PUTTING PERSUASION TO WORK

Now that you know about the type of language that works well in a persuasive essay, you need to look at how best to put that persuasive language to work.

THE BEST ORDER TO PERSUADE

When you are writing a persuasive essay, you are setting out to build a powerful case – one that no one will feel able to contradict.

You need to think about the personality you are projecting here. To win over your readers, it is wise to present yourself as a sensible, reasonable character, and sensible, reasonable characters are always aware that other people might have opposing views. So how do you deal with them? Just ignore them and hope they'll go away? That might make you appear ignorant and unaware of the world around you. Your structure needs to consider how best to deal with these contrary views and build in a way of defusing them. Here is a possible structural framework:

- You write an **introduction** that clearly sets out the topic's importance and significance before you make your viewpoint on it abundantly clear.
- You **acknowledge** that a conflict might exist, but you **reject** it in a reasonable, but brief, way. (Avoid being aggressive or offensive.)
- Launch your **first persuasive paragraph**.
- Continue with **similarly persuasive paragraphs**, saving your **strongest argument** until last.
- Write a **conclusion** in which you draw together again your main arguments from the body of the essay, ending perhaps with some stirring use of rising rhetorical triads.

WHAT DOES THIS LOOK LIKE IN PRACTICE?

This extract is from the opening paragraph of a persuasive essay. The writer is making the case that there is a need to limit the number of reality television programmes.

> *Reality television: time for another eviction*
>
> *When Channel 4, faced with disastrous ratings back in 2000, decided to revive its flagging fortunes, 'Big Brother' was born, Britain's first brush with so-called reality tv. A group of house-mates are kept under close observation until their number is whittled down through a public vote on candidates for eviction. The formula has evolved, however, (if that is the right term) to take in mindless variants such as 'The Only Way Is Essex' and 'Made in Chelsea' where the self-centred antics of a particular group are followed in a less restricted environment. The result is a form of soap opera which follows the sad lives of the socially challenged. With every new title the 'reality' seems to be further corrupted and divorced from genuine reality. Furthermore, the participants, who were originally chosen for their ordinariness, are now claiming inflated celebrity status for their highly questionable 'talents'. What kind of example is this setting for young people, undermining as it does the values of hard work and education? Surely the time has come to limit the insidious creep of this so-called reality on our television screens and celebrate real achievements in real life.*

- In the **title**, the persuasive slant of what is to come is made quite clear.
- In the **first four sentences**, the topic is defined, but in unashamedly emotive language.
- In the **fifth and sixth sentences**, two main reasons for the writer's unhappiness with the genre are made clear. These will form the material for development in the essay.
- Further reasons for criticism are hinted at in the **final two sentences**, pointing to the viewpoint to which the writer wishes to move us towards.

DON'T FORGET

Always keep your most persuasive argument until last. Make sure your essay builds to a powerful climax.

KEEPING UP THE PERSUASION

Once you have written an introduction to your persuasive essay that is rich in emotive language and other persuasive techniques, you need to **keep up** the persuasive pressure. Don't let your essay lapse into a list of shortcomings of reality television. Ensure that each subsequent paragraph is similarly persuasive in the way it addresses the reader.

One way to do this is to ensure there is evidence to back up claims already made. If you are going to develop the statement that reality television glorifies celebrity and undermines the need for hard work and education (in young people's eyes), you need to produce some evidence. And then, for good measure, you need to add a commentary to explain to the reader the implications that this evidence has. (You also need to remember to use emotive language.) Here's how you could do that.

Statement	Unattractive as some of the characters we meet in 'reality' television may be, that is not the most worrying issue. Much more disturbing is the fact that some young people are beginning to think that chasing 'celebrity' may be more worthwhile than hard work and education. Why, they are beginning to ask themselves, should I slog away at work, when I could 'just be myself' on reality television? Girls, perhaps, suffer most, being seen merely as attractive objects in this 'laddish' culture.
Evidence	According to Sarah Cassidy, an education journalist reviewing a recent poll, 'Ten percent of British teenagers say they would abandon their chances of a good education if they could become a star on reality television.' American lawyer Lisa Bloom goes further. She is concerned for the negative effect it has on girls in particular. 'This addiction to celebrity culture is creating a generation of dumbed-down women.'
Commentary	So, not only are young people being encouraged to think that **dedication to study and a career is a waste of their time**, they are being exposed to screen behaviour that is often **highly destructive to personality**, particularly to girls. This surely is indefensible? Haven't we had enough of this? Our young people deserve better role-models than those they see on 'reality' television.

THINGS TO DO AND THINK ABOUT

Make sure your final paragraph builds to a stirring climax, otherwise your persuasive efforts will fall rather flat. Think of how music often builds in power in its final bars. That's what your essay should do in the conclusion. Unleash the full force of rhetorical techniques here!

WORKING WITH PERSUASION

Here are some activities that will prepare you to write persuasive essays.

ACTIVITY 1

WHERE DO I STAND ON THIS ISSUE?

Think of an issue such as out-of-town shopping malls. You could either debate that they are essential and should be developed or that they are a blight on the landscape and should be limited. You could make several points on either side of the debate. If you want to carry out some research before you decide on your own viewpoint, then go to **www.idebate.org/debatabase** and scroll down to the 'Environment' topic. Decide on which side of the debate you stand then use the information to write the introduction to your persuasive essay on the topic.

Points for malls	Points against malls
Malls are good for competition and serve customers well. (The sheer size of many large stores ensures bulk purchasing brings good pricing.)	Out-of-town malls are bad for the environment. (Yet more acres and acres of ugly buildings.)
Out-of-town malls bring development to the area. (Other businesses tend to spring up around them to tap into their customer base.)	Out-of-town malls damage town centres. (High Street stores go out of business when trade moves to malls.)
Out-of-town malls offer a better shopping experience. (Full of light, colour, music, restaurants and cinemas. Shoppers are sheltered from bad weather.)	Out-of-town centres are bad for community identities. (Anonymous, faceless places, no relationships built up.)

Make sure your introduction uses emotive language, persuasive features and suggests in its closing sentence(s) the areas your persuasive essay will cover. Keep it brief: 150–200 words.

ACTIVITY 2

HOW WELL DID I DO? (1)

Once you have completed your introduction, swap it with a partner. Ask them to check it out according to the following points. As well as giving a mark out of 5, ask them to comment on each feature. Do they have suggestions to make to improve the content?

Features	Mark out of 5	Comment
Effective definition of topic?		
Viewpoint made clear?		
Use of emotive language?		
Use of persuasive techniques?		
Clear road-map?		

DON'T FORGET

It's easy enough to remember to be persuasive in the introduction, but you need to keep it going throughout the essay.

ACTIVITY 3

ADDING THE PERSUASIVE ANGLE

Here is a weak attempt at the introduction to a persuasive essay. The writer wishes to persuade us that governments should restrict advertising aimed at children. Information is very basic and there is little here that sounds persuasive. Rewrite it, retaining the basic information but adding an emotive element to the language, as many persuasive features as you judge appropriate and a hint of the points that will be developed. Should you wish to supplement the information here, go to **www.idebate.org/debatabase** and then to No 46 of the Top 100 Debates. Write 150–200 words.

Advertising that is aimed at children is bad. It gets them to eat junk food and demand things from their parents. We have restricted advertising for cigarettes and that seems to have worked. Kids, after all, don't really know what is good for them and they make a nuisance of themselves by asking for stuff their parents might not be able to afford.

ACTIVITY 4

ENDING WELL

Here is a proposed ending for the essay in Activity 3. The student's skills here seem just as weak as they were in the introduction. Rewrite, adding emotive language and persuasive features that build to a fine, emotive climax at the end. Go back and check out the list of persuasive features on page 70. Pay particular attention to repetition, parallel structures and rising rhetorical triads. These are powerful tools in writing your conclusion. Has this student left the most powerful argument to last? If you feel this has not been done, adjust the order.

So we have seen that some advertisers make money from children but the children are left with bad teeth and are often fat as a result of eating sugary, fatty foods. These are maybe problems for life. If we stopped cigarette advertising on television, we could do the same with advertising of sweets and soft drinks. We should stop advertising to children because it damages their health, it asks them to make decisions about matters they do not fully understand and causes problems for their parents.

ACTIVITY 5

HOW WELL DID I DO? (2)

As you did in Activity 2, swap your re-write with a partner and get their review of your conclusion. As well as giving a mark out of 5, ask them to comment on each feature. Do they have suggestions to make to improve the content?

Features	Mark out of 5	Comment
Main points touched on again?		
Emotive language?		
Persuasive features?		
Successful climax?		

THINGS TO DO AND THINK ABOUT

Make sure you support your points with evidence. This can come from experts, publications or polls. A persuasive essay without support of any kind tends to be rather unconvincing.

ARGUMENTATIVE ESSAY

Definition: the objective presentation of an issue or topic

Purpose: to inform; to analyse

Features	Style/language
• Sets out two sides of an argument without bias. • Presents balanced evidence for both sides. • Might/might not decide for one side after full exploration of evidence.	• Formal in tone. • Avoidance of personal pronouns. • Unemotional, reasoned language. • Use of 'authority' to support arguments.

+ DON'T FORGET

It helps the reader if you make the final sentence in your introduction (to argumentative persuasive and critical essays) indicate the **order** in which you are going to tackle your material; a roadmap, so to speak: *To understand fully what is at stake here, we must first examine <u>why CCTV can be seen as a useful tool</u> in the fight against crime and then consider <u>why some see it as a serious invasion of privacy</u>.* In this way, readers are prepared for what's to come.

WHAT MAKES AN ARGUMENTATIVE ESSAY DIFFERENT FROM A PERSUASIVE ESSAY?

Like a persuasive essay, an argumentative essay takes a controversial topic about which people might hold passionately different views as its starting point. There are major differences, however.

- There is no attempt to win over readers by emotive vocabulary or persuasive devices. Where the persuasive essay is often **informal** and chatty in tone, the argumentative essay is always **formal** in tone and vocabulary.
- Where the persuasive essay is **subjective** in its approach to the topic – that is, the very personal views of the writer are being presented, the argumentative essay is **objective** in its attitude to the topic – that is, the information is examined in purely factual terms with no personal slant colouring its presentation.

The text box above lays out some of the major language features of the argumentative essay. To see these in action, take a look now at how the title of and introduction to an argumentative essay can differ from those of a persuasive one.

Argumentative approach	Persuasive approach
University education: to pay or not to pay?	**Why university education must be free**
While primary and secondary education in this country are freely available to all, university education now comes at a variable but often substantial cost, depending on the choice of university. It was in 1998 that the then Labour government introduced the concept of student tuition fees for the first time. This move saw the nation divided: universities and some politicians argued that fees were necessary to safeguard courses and to maintain standards in an increasingly competitive global education market; students and certain politicians pointed out that any additional cost to young people at this stage in their career would see interest in university education diminishing. In the intervening years, fees have risen steadily, with reasons for and against the increases further dividing opinion. This essay will examine the effects of the introduction of fees in the period since 1998 from the viewpoint of both university managers and university students, with the aim of determining whether university education should come at a cost to the student or not.	In this country, there was once a proud tradition of free university education. In fact, under the old grants system, students were paid good money by the state to pursue tertiary education. The student benefited; the state benefited. Britain enjoyed a source of highly educated professionals; students set out on a debt-free future. How times have changed! Now we're hearing horror stories of students leaving university with debts running into tens of thousands of pounds. What encouragement is this for our brightest and best secondary pupils to apply for university? Why start out on a career with a crippling debt burden of this kind? And how many pupils simply decide university is not for them? If the nation does not wish to suffer this kind of intellectual haemorrhaging, we surely need to make university education free for all. In this way, interest in university education flourishes, students study unencumbered by financial nightmares and the nation benefits from a university-educated workforce. Where is the downside in all this?

RECOGNISING FORMAL TONE

When you are writing an argumentative essay you need to use a formal approach to maintain your neutral analysis of the arguments of both sides. The example on p76 uses a formal tone. But how **exactly** does formal tone show itself in a written text? How does it differ from the informal or colloquial tone in persuasive writing? Here are some recurring features.

Sentence length

In persuasive writing you will often encounter minor sentences or even one word sentences. Formal writing avoids such sentence styles and tends to use compound or complex sentences (see pages 21–25 to remind yourself about them). As a result, sentences tend to be longer in formal texts, and are often composed of several subordinate clauses.

Avoidance of personal pronouns

To remain neutral, remove any features that suggest personal involvement with the topic – so be wary of using 'I', 'you' or 'we'. The use of the third-person narrative style reinforces this formality of tone – for example: *the nation needs ...* rather than *we need ...*

Avoidance of abbreviations

Informal writing often uses personal pronouns and also abbreviated forms of words attached to them: *we're ... we can't ... I've...* Avoid these features in formal writing to emphasise a certain detachment from the topic. You should also avoid *it's ... there's ... that's ... doesn't ... couldn't ....* They all add an informal chattiness to the text which is alien to formal tone.

Avoidance of colloquial expressions/words

Words and expressions which you might use talking to friends are not really appropriate for the tone you wish to set up in an argumentative essay. Instead of:

Their analysis is basically OK but they seem to have got the wrong end of the stick when they get round to taking a look at living costs.

Formal tone prefers something like:

Their analysis is basically sound but there are possibly certain errors in their discussion of living costs.

You may find yourself using quite a number of the Latin/Greek-sourced words we worked with earlier such as *contradict, empathise, regress, subscribe* and *retract.*

Avoidance of informal commands

In informal persuasive writing you might have sentences which begin with informal commands such as:

<u>Imagine</u> how you would ... <u>Consider</u> for a minute what ... <u>Don't wait</u> for ...

By writing like this, you are talking to a reader in terms of the second-person 'you'. Formal writing prefers third-person narrative style:

It takes little imagination to imagine how students would react to ... Even a brief consideration might ... It is perhaps not wise to wait until ...

Avoidance of exclamations and rhetorical questions

If you are writing formally, avoid the emotional exclamations of anger, excitement or surprise that you might be tempted to indulge in when writing persuasively. A text peppered with exclamation marks and question marks is far from being detached in its approach to its subject matter.

In putting forward a reasoned case, however, consider the usefulness of punctuation marks such as the colon and semi-colon.

DON'T FORGET

Always make a final check of your argumentative essay to ensure that no evaluative adjectives or phrases of your own have accidentally slipped into your presentation of facts.

THINGS TO DO AND THINK ABOUT

Formality of tone is traditional in argumentative writing. Look back at the guidelines in this section to check that you have written formally throughout an argumentative essay. You could also get a partner to read through your draft to check for any informality that might have crept in.

SETTING OUT YOUR ARGUMENTS

Arguments should be presented in such a way that the reader is carried effortlessly and smoothly through them. There should be no unexplained, sudden or puzzling changes of direction. Orderly sequencing of arguments is vital in making a convincing case. So, how do you organise a seamless flow of ideas?

One way would be to examine your evidence and then decide where your final verdict falls: are you for or against an idea?

For example, if you were **for** there being university fees of some sort, you might usefully consider the following order of presentation:

- An **introduction** that sets out both sides, but places the **positive** second.
- **Subsequent paragraphs/sections** that deal with the **negative** side of fees.
- **Paragraphs/sections** that look at the **benefits** to be derived from fees.
- **A summative conclusion** making clear where you stand on university fees – that is, in favour.

WHY USE THIS ORDER?

Suppose you are in favour of university fees but leave discussing their drawbacks until the second half of your essay. Think of the effect on your reader if you abruptly announce in the **concluding** paragraph that you are in favour of something that only a few lines previously you have been expertly criticising. You will puzzle and disconcert them: one minute you are pointing out the shortcomings of an issue, the next you are saying you are in favour of it.

So what comes first?

If you are in favour of a topic, discuss its negative points earlier in the essay, so that your positive case seamlessly precedes your positive conclusion. The reader will not have forgotten your negative points, but the positive ones will be fresher in their mind and your approval of them will seem all the more understandable and logical.

The reverse also holds good: if you are **against** an issue, acknowledge its benefits first and then discuss its shortcomings afterwards, so that you lead into a conclusion that follows naturally on from these shortcomings.

Remember the need for evidence

We have already mentioned the key role played by evidence in persuasive writing in supporting your case and giving it authority. In an argumentative essay, the need for evidence is just as great – perhaps even more so – because here you are presenting not a subjective opinion but an objective case. This evidence can come from a variety of sources: acknowledged subject experts, quality journals, newspapers and magazines or polls. But don't just quote the author and leave matters there – discuss what you think the implications are and show yourself to be an effective analyst.

The need for a conclusion

The conclusion summarises the main points of the two sides involved. If you decide to withhold an opinion of your own then that's a perfectly legitimate position to take up – just make sure that you have good reasons for doing so, and that you make these reasons clear – otherwise you risk looking like a ditherer and your essay will limp to a halt.

BEWARE PLAGIARISM!

When you are carrying out research for your argumentative and persuasive essays, you will probably look for information in sources such as quality journals and newspapers, recognised websites, published polls and government statistics. But when you take notes, be careful not to accidentally plagiarise by 'lifting' expert opinion without correctly acknowledging the source. Avoid this by using a coloured highlighter to flag up direct quotes in your notes – this will remind you that somebody else wrote this and that these are the person's actual words. (Note the source of the quotation and mention this either directly underneath the quotation or in the bibliography at the end of the essay.) Even if you paraphrase the comment of an expert, always give the source.

CITING SOURCES

You must always acknowledge your sources. The occasional quotation in an essay can be acknowledged as you cite it.

EXAMPLE

Writing in the January 2015 edition of 'The Lancet', Professor John MacPherson claims that …

But if you are quoting from a lot of sources, it is probably more sensible to acknowledge them in a bibliography at the end of your essay. (But to avoid any confusion, say at least who said this in the body of your essay.)

Learning to set out sources properly will be useful when you go on to college or university.

There are several recognised ways of setting out sources. The following one is known as APA style (American Psychological Association) and is commonly used in British academic institutions.

Referencing books

Here is how to reference books in the APA style:

Surname of author first, then initial. (follow by the year of publication in brackets) *then comes the title in italics.* Then the city of publication: and finally the publisher.

A complete book reference should appear like this:

King, R. (2000) *Brunelleschi's Dome.* London: Penguin.

A list of books in your bibliography should be organised alphabetically by author's surname.

Referencing newspapers and magazine articles

Here is how to reference articles from newspapers or magazines:

Surname of the author first, then initial. (follow by the publication date in brackets) Next include the title of the article itself. *Then the name of the publication should come in italics.* And finally the page reference.

A complete article reference should appear like this:

Goring, R. (4 January 2003) She's Talking Our Language Now. *The Herald.* p.14.

Referencing electronically sourced material

Here is how to reference electronically sourced material:

Give the name of author (if available) and title of article/ publication as you would for a print publication. In place of city of publication and name of publisher, put the web address and the date when the article was posted (if available) and also the date when you accessed it.

DON'T FORGET

Have a few synonyms up your sleeve for the conclusion of your discursive essays. Yes, you are summing up information you have mentioned previously, but a change of vocabulary avoids boring your reader with repetition and gives a fresh look to the discussion.

THINGS TO DO AND THINK ABOUT

Don't be frightened to disagree with expert witnesses you have cited. You are entitled to your own view! Just be careful to criticise neutrally – appeal to contrary **facts** rather than contrary **emotions**. If you do this in a calm and measured way, then it suggests that you are an independent thinker – never a bad thing.

APPROACHING THE ARGUMENTATIVE

Here are some activities that will prepare you to write argumentative essays.

ACTIVITY 1

PRACTISING WITH FORMAL TONE (1)

Here is part of a persuasive text in which the tone is informal and chatty, but the writer is clearly angry about the use of young children in sweatshops. Rewrite the paragraph in what you feel is a more formal tone, taking care to maintain the basic information and opinion of the original writer. (Refer back to page 77 for the guidelines.)

These sweat shops in the Far East really are the limit! Think for a minute: these poor wee kids are expected to work all the hours that God sends just to make fancy trainers for us in the West. Would they not be better off in school learning the three Rs and messing about with paints and pianos? We in the West need to get off our backsides and do something about this ASAP instead of mouthing off about it in posh newspapers.

ACTIVITY 2

PRACTISING WITH FORMAL TONE (2)

Here the writer is again using an informal, chatty tone to discuss a topic. Re-write the paragraph in a formal and objective tone, using the guidelines outlined on page 77.

> So if politicians really want to do something about stopping some teenagers drinking themselves senseless, they need to tell supermarkets where they get off. It's no good giving pubs a bad time about under-age drinking if, once chucked out, the same guys can get their big brother to nip into a supermarket for their favourite tipple. And get it a whole lot cheaper! Until pubs and supermarkets are both singing the same tune and upping prices so it hurts, the politicians are strictly up the creek without a paddle on this one.

ACTIVITY 3

ORGANISING AN INTRODUCTION

Here are some rough notes jotted down by a student for an argumentative essay on Closed-Circuit Television (CCTV). Some of these facts/comments (in no particular order) could be useful in the introduction to this essay. Select **only** information that you consider to be relevant for an introduction to an argumentative essay. Organise the facts to form a coherent introduction. Always keep your tone formal.

Remember, this is the introduction to an argumentative essay, so you should not take sides – just give the reader an idea of what CCTV is, its significance in the world and the two opposed views to its use. You could also, perhaps, hint at the way your essay will develop.

Remember: you **don't** need to use all this information – you only need to make a selection.

contd

ACTIVITY 3 CONT.

The student intended the title to be:
Closed-Circuit Television: friend or foe?

- *Product of 'nanny state'. Big brother always watching you.*
- *First CCTV installed in 1942 by Siemens in Peenemunde, Germany, to oversee the launch of Hitler's V-2 rockets.*
- *Useful tool in fight against crime.*
- *CCTV is surveillance by cameras to transmit an image to a central control to monitor security in places where security might be an issue: commercial streets, airports, car parks, supermarkets, public transport etc.*
- *Britain said to have more CCTV cameras than any other European country.*
- *2009 report by Cambridge University found them most effective in car parks where crime was reduced by 51 per cent. In public transport, crime reduced by 23 per cent.*
- *Serious invasion of privacy. No place in free country.*
- *Keeps our streets safe.*
- *A 2008 report by UK Police Chiefs concluded that only 3 per cent of crimes were solved by CCTV. So cost-effective?*

ACTIVITY 4

PEER REVIEWING INTRODUCTIONS

Once you have completed your introduction to the argumentative essay on CCTV, exchange it with a partner. Ask them to comment on this paragraph, using the following grid to help focus their thoughts.

Feature	Mark out of 5	Comment
Significance/importance of topic made apparent?		
Argument 'against' clearly expressed?		
Argument 'for' clearly expressed?		
Formal tone respected throughout?		
'Road-map' suggesting way essay will develop?		

If you find there are weaknesses in any particular section of the introduction, go back and rewrite it in the light of your partner's comments. Have you managed to improve it?

ACTIVITY 5

GOING ONE STEP FURTHER

After reviewing your introduction to the argumentative essay on CCTV:

- decide on which side of the argument you stand
- then write **one** paragraph supporting **one** of your arguments.

If you need more evidence to support the focus of this particular paragraph, key:

'After Boston: the pros and cons of surveillance cameras'

into your browser. This will give you an authoritative and balanced article by CNN reporter Heather Kelly.

This paragraph outline may help you keep on task:

Statement(s)/ topic sentence	Make clear at once what this paragraph is to be about. This could take the form of a single topic sentence or a series of sentences stating in very general terms what you are going to cover.
Evidence	This is where you produce evidence in the form of a comment(s) by a subject expert, or a quotation(s) from an article or a statistics-based report to support the claim(s) made in your opening statement/topic sentence: *According to a Metropolitan Police report in 2008, only 3% of crimes were solved by ... Added to this is the figure of ... A further report by Manchester Police indicated that ...*
Commentary	Now that you have found this interesting evidence, you need to make it work for you. Explain for the reader what the implications of this comment/ statistic are: *Comments and statistics such as these might lead some to raise questions as to the cost-effectiveness of a system which ...*

ACTIVITY 6

HOW WELL DID I DO?

Again, invite a partner to read through and comment on your paragraph for Activity 5. They can use this grid to help them focus their thoughts.

Feature	Mark out of 5	Checklist for peer review
Statement(s)/ topic sentence		Was there here a clearly focused expression of what this particular paragraph was to be about? Did the writer lay out a **single** topic for discussion – for example, cost? human rights? efficiency? Or did they muddle up various points in a single paragraph?
Evidence		Did the writer produce evidence sufficiently convincing to back up the point raised in their opening statement(s)? Was there enough of it? Was the source made sufficiently clear?
Commentary		Did the writer unpack the evidence for the reader – that is, did they explain the implications of any figures/facts that were produced as evidence?
Tone		Was all the above expressed in the formal language that we looked at earlier in this section? Or did emotive language and persuasive devices creep in?

CRITICAL ESSAY

Definition: a formal piece of writing presenting a reasoned answer to a set question

Purpose: to explain, analyse and evaluate information

Features	Style/language
• Focuses clearly on a specific question. • Uses textual evidence to support analytical response. • Demonstrates personal engagement with text. • Arguments framed by introduction and conclusion.	• Formal in tone. • Third-person narrative for explanations and analysis. • 'I' or 'we' for personal response. • Technical/analytical vocabulary.

WHY WRITE A CRITICAL ESSAY?

The critical essay is an interesting combination of the formal, analytical approach you adopt for an argumentative essay and the personal engagement you bring to a reflective essay.

Overall, you are demonstrating your ability to engage with a set question and to produce and interpret textual evidence in response to the question, before revealing a personal response in your evaluation.

The tone is formal as you explain and analyse what is going on in the text. The narrative normally uses the third person:

> **EXAMPLE**
>
> In attempting to capture the mood of the storm, the poet makes considerable use of technical poetic devices such as alliteration and onomatopoeia. When he describes the wind in the trees outside he ...

When evaluating the evidence you put forward, a more personal note produces a good effect; the pronouns 'I', 'me' 'we' or 'us' are often to be found here, as are possessive adjectives such as 'my' and 'our':

> **EXAMPLE**
>
> By sustained use of such devices, we as readers find that we can almost hear the water washing the pebbles against each other. But it is not just our sense of hearing which is being appealed to; we seem to see the ripples, too, in our imagination when ...

Choose a play in which the playwright presents a flawed character who you feel is more worthy of our sympathy than criticism.

By referring to appropriate techniques, show how the character's flawed nature is revealed, then explain how, despite this, we are led to feel sympathy for her/him.

READING THE QUESTION

A good answer shows an obvious understanding of what the question wants as a response. So the first thing you need to do is to break down the wording of the question, so you know what it's asking. Suppose you were faced with this question:

- 'presents a flawed character' and 'show how the character's flawed nature is revealed' needs to be considered. Not a bad character, nor an entirely good one either but one with a flaw. You will need to say clearly early on **what** this flaw is: too ambitious, too trusting, too sensual?

- You will need also to think about how the playwright 'presents' this character 'by referring to appropriate techniques'. **How** is he/she presented: by contrasting him/her with another character? By the language used by the character? By behaviour towards others? By what others say of him/her? By the imagery surrounding him/her?

- The phrases 'who you feel is more worthy of our sympathy than criticism' and 'we are led to feel sympathy' are asking you for a personal response to this character. You can't just claim sympathy and leave it there – you need to point to the evidence that brings out your sympathy. **Why** exactly are you feeling sympathy? Have you got evidence that shows the character in a really positive light – for example, do they perform generous acts, or do you have evidence that their 'flaw' is not typical of their normal behaviour, or that they are under unusual and extreme pressure?

If you take time to think carefully about the wording of the question and jot down points (and supporting evidence) that you can use to answer it, you will be well on track for a successful essay.

Whatever the question, always double-check that you have looked at **all** the keywords in the way we have here. Read the question through completely first and don't just pounce on the first keywords you come to and set to work on them.

PLANNING A RESPONSE

Now that you have jotted down all the points you **might** want to make, you need to plan and organise these points so that they will form a coherent structure. You normally have a time limit for essays of this kind, so that means that perhaps not all the points you first thought of can be included. You now need to do some planning, and perhaps some pruning:

- Which points are you going to include?
- Have you enough time to make this number of points?
- In which order are you going to present them?
- Have you sufficient evidence to support the selected points?

Some people like to plan by making lists, others like to draw mind-maps. The actual format selected for your plan is less important than the fact that you actually **do** have a plan if you are to make best use of limited time. The plan keeps you on task and stops you getting sidetracked. Usually, you will find that the number of major points you want to make equates with the number of body paragraphs you are setting yourself to write for the core of the essay. This number can vary, but three or four major points will normally be sufficient for the body paragraphs for an essay of 45 minutes.

DON'T FORGET

As with a persuasive essay, when you are making a case in a critical essay start with a good point, follow it with a better one and keep your very best one until last. This helps your essay build in persuasiveness as it advances towards a convincing climax. Think carefully about the quality of each point as you plan.

THINGS TO DO AND THINK ABOUT

You will often write a critical essay as part of a timed assessment. Don't let time pressure panic you into writing before you have completed the following quick mental checklist:

- Given the text(s) I have studied, is this **really** the best choice of question for me?
- Have I studied **all** the wording of the question and not just a few keywords of it?
- Does my plan match up **fully** to the demands of the question?
- Given the time available, is my plan a realistic one?
- Do I have sufficient evidence to support the opening statements or topic sentences in each paragraph?

STRUCTURING YOUR CRITICAL ESSAY

STRUCTURING YOUR INTRODUCTION

A good introduction should suggest to the marker that you have planned your answers intelligently and that your knowledge of the text is thorough. Here's a checklist for a successful introduction:

- State the **title of the selected text** (in inverted commas!) and its **author** clearly in your first sentence. In the same sentence, adopt some wording which suggests that you have chosen this text because it fits the set question.

So in response to the SQA-style question, you might write:

> 'Macbeth' by William Shakespeare presents us with a flawed character in the person of King Duncan. Although Macbeth himself is the most seriously flawed character in the play, King Duncan, whom Macbeth murders to mount the throne, is someone who is also flawed but reveals himself to be more worthy of our sympathy than criticism.

- Follow this with a brief **summary** – four or five lines – of the action of the play.

> In this play, Macbeth, a much admired and successful general is spurred on by ambition to murder his king, Duncan, to become ruler of Scotland. It soon becomes clear that his progressive descent into tyranny – and ultimately death – stems from his initial murder of the sympathetic but weak Duncan.

- Now revisit the wording of the second part of the question to assure the examiner that you have not forgotten about that second part.

> Shakespeare reveals the flaws in Duncan's nature by the technique of associating him thematically with the dangers of trust in a very dangerous world. We see his country being invaded by his clearly untrustworthy neighbours; we see the man being taken in not once but twice by the false appearance of his courtiers. Shakespeare's use of dramatic irony in Duncan's acts of generosity to a man and woman who are plotting his death underlines his gullibility. Yet our sympathy for him is seen in these very acts of personal generosity towards those around him and in the imagery of growth and fertility which surrounds him, imagery which is the very opposite of that associated with Macbeth.

Note that we are not just a refering **back** to the question but also refering **forward** to our 'road-map' for the essay: a discussion of how Shakespeare uses incidents at national and personal levels to indicate flaws in character; the use of dramatic irony; an exploration of the connotations of imagery to show Duncan's attractiveness.

STRUCTURING BODY PARAGRAPHS

In the final stages of our introduction, our 'road-map' hinted at a structure of perhaps four body paragraphs in our essay.

Each of these four paragraphs needs to be headed by a clear **statement** of the point you are setting out to demonstrate to your reader. Sometimes this is called a topic sentence, but sometimes you might want to write more than a single sentence to make your point clear.

Statement

> One of Shakespeare's methods for retaining our sympathy for Duncan is his frequent underlining of his natural generosity. There is both generosity of spirit and generosity of action in his responses to the world around him. In this, he is in marked contrast to Macbeth whose natural reaction is often marked by suspicion of others.

This topic sentence or series of sentences then needs to be followed by **evidence** to support this claim about Duncan. This requires either direct reference to incidents in the play or quotations from the play.

Evidence

> When news of the battles threatening his kingdom is brought to him by a blood-stained messenger, Duncan's generosity of spirit is evident when he personally summons help for him, saying:
>
> > 'Go get him surgeons.'
>
> When the victorious Macbeth returns from his successful defence of the nation, Duncan's generous response is immediate: he rewards him by creating him Thane of Cawdor. Lady Macbeth, too, receives a gift of a diamond. To others of Macbeth's household, Duncan has 'sent forth great largess'.

But we cannot simply present evidence and leave readers to make what they will of it. We need to unpack it for them a little, explaining what the implications of all this are by giving a brief **commentary** on it.

Commentary

> Overall, we can see that this is a great-hearted man. That a king in a moment of national crisis should personally see to the needs of a humble soldier does much to arouse our sympathy for the man. His prompt reward to an able general is a most generous one, with no thought to how this able general might pose a threat to him. In his ironic gift of a diamond to the woman whose murder plot will end his life a few hours later, we see a man who responds generously to those who serve him. This shows his fundamental decency, which elicits our sympathy when he falls victim to the Macbeths. It also reveals, however, that this unquestioning trust and generosity can be at the same time a serious flaw in the dangerous times in which he lives.

STRUCTURING A CONCLUSION

A good essay needs a good conclusion. It doesn't need to be all that long, but it does need to perform certain tasks to secure your standing as a credible commentator on literature.

Here are a few guidelines:

- The first sentence of this concluding paragraph should refer back to some wording of the question itself. Here you are reminding the marker you have kept to the original task, for example: 'Standing back from the text as a whole, we see that Duncan is a flawed character but one who retains our sympathy largely because ...'
- You should go on to sum up **briefly** the main points you have been making in the central section of your essay.
- **Do not** bring in new points or quotations at this late stage. It will only spoil the sharp focus of the case you have been making throughout your essay.

DON'T FORGET

A good tip in a conclusion is to have a number of synonyms up your sleeve for keywords mentioned in your introduction. This will add variety to your summing up by avoiding verbal repetition.

THINGS TO DO AND THINK ABOUT

When writing a critical essay, always keep checking that each paragraph is responding in some way to the question. No amount of clever comment will make up for the fact that you have lost sight of the question.

USING QUOTATIONS IN YOUR CRITICAL ESSAY

LONGER QUOTATIONS

There is more than one way to introduce a long quotation to your paragraph.

Describe it

Use a colon (:) then drop a line, indent slightly and begin the quotation using inverted commas – for example:

Her clear-sighted sadness is seen in the words:

> 'I have betrayed a great man and his like will never be seen again.'

Introduce it

In this case, the colon would only interrupt the natural flow of the words. Instead you should write:

Her clear-sighted sadness is seen when she comments that she has 'betrayed a great man and his like will never be seen again.'

Always make sure your longer quotations have room to breathe – drop a line (with or without a colon), indent slightly and add quotation marks. Drop another line before continuing your own text.

SHORTER QUOTATIONS

A good essay will have a mixture of longer and shorter quotations. Shorter ones can be just as effective as longer ones. If you can't remember the full quotation, you can use the parts you do remember to great effect.

For example, if you wanted to use the following quotation:

'the street shone out in contrast to its dingy neighbourhood, like a fire in a forest'

but you couldn't quite remember it in full, you could use the phrases you do remember to good effect and paraphrase the rest:

The street is described as making a sharp contrast to its 'dingy neighbourhood' and standing out 'like a fire in a forest'.

As long as you weave the short quotations seamlessly into your own text, this kind of paraphrase-plus-

quotation will prove more effective than a longer, misquoted extract. It could also pinpoint more sharply the exact point you wish to make.

GIVING A CONTEXT

Never assume that readers understand more than they do. No quotation, however well chosen, will have its desired effect unless you give it a brief **context**. In other words, indicate briefly not just who said it, but why and under what circumstances.

If, for instance, you had been reading *Macbeth* and wanted to make a comment about King Duncan's generosity of nature, you might want to mention his kindness to a wounded messenger – but be careful how you do it.

✗ Duncan shows he has a great generosity of nature: 'Go get him surgeons.'

✓ Duncan has a great generosity of nature. Seeing a badly-wounded messenger collapse, he personally orders him to be taken care of: 'Go get him surgeons.'

A context does not need to be long – it simply needs to lead readers into the quotation in a way that helps them make sense of the point you are making.

WRITING AN EFFECTIVE LEAD-IN

Make sure your lead-in to the quotation does not simply repeat the content of the quotation.

For example, in this description of the landscape in *Scotland* – a poem by Alexander Gray – a poor lead-in might be:

The poet regards the trees and wonders if they are trees or just bushes:

> 'Or are they but bushes?'

Such empty repetition does not really help the reader to understand the point the poet is getting at here.

A better lead-in might be:

So seriously stunted are the trees by the winds that constantly seem to rage around them in this harsh Scottish landscape, the poet is prompted to question their identity as trees at all:

> 'Or are they but bushes?'

In other words, a thoughtful lead-in does more than simply help readers to understand the quotation's context – it can also underline your ability to evaluate the quotation's significance.

CRITICAL ESSAY CHECKLIST

- You must select **only** the information from your text knowledge that answers the specific question in front of you. ☐

- You must be alert to all sections of the question and plan your time accordingly. ☐

- You need a plan that is more than just a loose collection of good points to help you structure a coherent essay. There should be a line of argument that holds the essay together from start to finish, with each paragraph being linked to the next. ☐

- Each paragraph should be carefully structured to ensure that your claims are supported by evidence and that you unpack this evidence for the reader. ☐

- When a question has a second part to it, inviting you to discuss 'central concerns' or to expand on how some aspect 'enhances your understanding of the text as a whole' or to comment on 'how it engages your interest in a portrayal', don't leave it all until the penultimate paragraph to discuss fully. You could leave yourself short of time. Instead, keep this discussion in sight by referring to it in **each paragraph**. You can then expand on it in the penultimate paragraph. ☐

- A soundly structured introduction will help you to stay on task, and a 'road-map' in the introduction's last sentence will help the marker to find their way round your arguments. A brief conclusion will remind them of your key points. ☐

- Use the correct procedure for laying out quotations, long or short. This shows good academic manners and attention to detail that increases your stature as a competent commentator on your texts. ☐

- Make sure your quotations make sense to someone who is not familiar with the text. That means checking that you have given each quotation a context, however brief. ☐

THINGS TO DO AND THINK ABOUT

Do not feel frustrated by the fact that assessment questions will always invite you to demonstrate only a fraction of your textual knowledge. It is the quality of your **selection** of relevant evidence that the marker is keen to see. Don't be tempted to offer critical points that are not relevant to the question, no matter how insightful they are.

DON'T FORGET

A well-focused short quote is always more effective than a long rambling one. It is easier to remember and also focuses precisely on the point you want to present to the marker.

PRACTICE FOR CRITICAL ESSAY WRITING

ACTIVITY 1

WORKING WITH INTRODUCTIONS (1)

Here is a past exam question for a critical essay on a poem. Without tackling the entire essay, attempt to structure an introduction to your essay in response to the question. Look back at the guidelines earlier in this section for structuring an introduction.

> Choose a poem which features an encounter or an incident.
>
> By referring to appropriate techniques, show how the poet's development of the encounter or incident leads you to a deeper understanding of the poem's central concerns.

Choose any poem that you have read recently which features an encounter or incident. There are quite a few around! Then write your introduction, checking if it matches the points raised in the grid below.

Points in your introduction	Example
Name the poem and author and match it to the wording of the question.	
Summarise what happens in the poem.	
Mention the techniques you will examine and say what the central concern(s) of the poem is.	

ACTIVITY 2

WORKING WITH INTRODUCTIONS (2)

Once you have completed your introduction, exchange it with a partner. Invite him/her to comment on the following points:

Features	Mark out of 5	Comments
How appropriate did your choice of poem seem for the question?		
Did you summarise the poem clearly and briefly? Did the summary make clear why this poem had been chosen?		
Did the end of your introduction make reference to the wording of the question's second sentence?		
How well did the end of the introduction indicate the course the essay will follow?		

ACTIVITY 3

WORKING WITH STATEMENTS, EVIDENCE AND COMMENTARY

Practise constructing a body paragraph using a story from your childhood. Here is a **statement** from an essay on *Little Red Riding Hood* which could form the opening of a body paragraph on the tale. Produce the **evidence** section and then give your **commentary** on this evidence.

contd

ACTIVITY 3 CONT.

You can probably cite the evidence from your childhood memory of the story. (In case you have forgotten the details, you can check it out at www.eastoftheweb.com – search for 'Brothers Grimm'.)

Little Red Riding Hood is someone who is not lacking in admirable qualities as a human being. She is both kind-hearted in offering to take food to her ailing grandmother and courageous in facing up to the wolf she encounters in the wood on the way. Sadly, however, her behaviour for much of the story suggests she is lacking in basic intelligence.

Now go on to give the evidence for this lack of 'basic intelligence' by referring directly to incidents in the story **or** using quotations from the tale **or** a mixture of both. Then go on to explain the implications of this evidence in your commentary for example: 'From remarks such as these it is clear to us that the child ...'

ACTIVITY 4

TURN YOUR STATEMENT/EVIDENCE/ COMMENTARY INTO A MINI ESSAY

As well as firming up the body paragraphs of your essay, this Statement/Evidence/Commentary construct can be used quite independently of any essay. For example, if you are revising for an exam, you can practise writing about any aspect of the play, poem or novel you are reading with this SEC construct.

First, think about the statement you want to make, then find the evidence for it. Finally, think about which point(s) you are going to make about the evidence in your commentary. Here are some general ideas to get you thinking about this writing practice. The more you write these, the surer your grasp of a full-scale essay will eventually be.

What makes Character X in your play, novel or poem a likeable person?	Suggest what setting contributes to the atmosphere in one section of your play, novel or poem.
How does the playwright arouse our interest in the opening scene of his play?	Suggest why a particular scene/ episode in your text is significant.
Why is Character X in conflict with one other character in the play/novel?	How does one episode or scene in your play, novel or poem help illustrate a major theme in the work?

ACTIVITY 5

WHAT PART OF THE ESSAY IS THIS?

Once you have worked on critical essay writing for some time, you begin to develop a sixth sense for the kind of language you need to use for the various sections in this kind of text. Here are some sections from essays by students. Study the way each one is written before saying if it sounds as if it comes from:

- an introduction
- body paragraph or
- conclusion.

If it belongs in a body paragraph, say whether it belongs in the Statement, Evidence or Commentary section.

Make sure you can explain why you placed your answer in the section you have chosen. What were the verbal clues in the text that helped you place the section?

1. *When we consider the evidence which I have discussed here, it is probably fair to say that, overall, this is a play in which evil is only partially triumphant. Admittedly ...*

2. *To determine the nature of the heroine's isolation, we need to examine her relations with her husband, her family and with the wider community ...*

3. *From comments such as these, it is clear that Hale is someone who has changed from the person he was when we first met him. Where, we wonder, is the man who believed that ...*

4. *In this novel the narrator is an overweight, aging novelist, struggling to finish the long-awaited follow-up to his award-winning novel. The narrative deals with his battle to complete his two-thousand-page masterpiece, 'Wonder Boys'.*

5. *Symbolism is yet another technique which Donovan employs to invoke our sympathy for the old lady.*

6. *A novel in which there is an unreliable narrator is 'The Confessions of a Justified Sinner' by James Hogg.*

7. *The poet delights in the sheer beauty of the day. The attention is first given to describing the air around him which he hears as being filled with lark song which rose 'on long thin strings of singing'. The heat haze is not just any heat haze but to him is 'the actual shimmer of angels', so wonderful is its subtle movement to him.*

THINGS TO DO AND THINK ABOUT

Each paragraph in your essay should target three aims: to show knowledge of what happens in the text; to offer specific textual evidence to back up this knowledge and to help the reader to realise what the implications of this evidence are.

Start writing, no matter what. The water does not flow until the tap is turned on. – Louis L'Amour

MASTERING WRITING SKILLS

You have now examined many of the skills you need to be a better writer. But to develop these skills, you need to practise them. If you make writing part of your regular study routine, you'll begin to see real progress. And so will your teachers.

MAKING A START

We know you have a lot of work to do for your other subjects. But better writing skills will benefit your performance in these subjects, too, so it is well worth setting aside time – no matter how short a time – to practise writing skills regularly. Here are some tips to help you.

Read with a critical eye

No matter what you enjoy reading – novels, newspapers, magazines, websites or whatever – read with a critical eye. That means examining **how** these professional writers kept you reading. Check out how they made a certain effect: interesting sentence structure, beginning with an anecdote, use of parallel structure, dramatic imagery. Pick up tips from the professionals and adapt the idea to suit your own work. That's how all professional writers started.

Get into the habit

Write a paragraph or two every day about a certain idea or topic. It might be a creative or discursive subject. It might simply be a diary entry. Keep writing without thinking too much about it. Then look at it critically. Did you demonstrate any of the skills we've been talking about here? If not, then go back and edit it. Add some of the technical effects you've been learning about to give it a polish.

Freewrite

Freewriting is an excellent way to get your writing moving when you might not be feeling too creative. Professor Peter Elbow is the great freewriting guru. Key 'Freewriting Peter Elbow' into your browser and read his brief article. Then put some of his ideas into action. You could be pleasantly surprised by the results you achieve! Some phrases or sentences could well form the basis of a more considered piece.

Shadow yourself

If you're stuck about what to write, look at your own day, but through the eyes of someone else – perhaps someone in fiction. Choose someone from one of the texts you have been reading recently in class. What would they make of your life? Would they envy you or feel sorry for you?

FINDING A WAY FORWARD

Your teachers might give you some direction about creative and discursive topics. Or you might be free to choose your own topic, although this sometimes poses problems. How can you get round them?

Check out the press

If you are looking to write a discursive piece, whether persuasive or discursive, the national 'heavyweight' press is a good place to start. There you'll find the hot topics of the day, written by top journalists. Not only will you find useful 'authority' for your points, but you might pick up some style tips too.

If you are looking for a plot for a creative piece, the local press could be a gold mine. Don't just take the story itself and the person(s) mentioned: Why did this event happen? Was anyone else involved whose name has not appeared perhaps? How did this incident affect the family? Change the names, of course! Take the bare bones and put some creative flesh on them.

Getting stuck

Writer's block happens to everyone. If this happens in a creative story, consult the character profile we suggested on page 52. Make some reference to a characteristic you noted as you pieced the character together. Maybe some reference to the setting might get you started again? If this still doesn't work, break off. Do something else. Tomorrow is another day and might bring its own solution.

In a discursive piece, tap some 'keywords' into your browser and see if the results bring up new material that you could use as the basis of another argument. If you are looking for a different angle on your topic, imagine how someone else might view this topic: your mother, the Prime Minister or any character from history.

If all fails in either a creative or discursive piece, move on to another part of your text that you feel more certain about. Work on that and then go back to the problem area. You will often find this brief change of focus can help recapture the flow.

THE FINAL POLISH

Here are a few tips for giving your draft a final polish.

Strong verbs, not adverbs

Many professional writers advise against the thoughtless use of adverbs, with one even suggesting that 'the road to hell is paved with adverbs.' This might be going a bit far. But the impact of *The goalkeeper slumped ...* seems a lot stronger than *The goalkeeper fell heavily ...* Strong verbs tend to give more impact than overused verbs supported by an adverb.

End-weighting

English is what is called an 'end-weighted' language – that is, the principal focus of a sentence is often retained until the end of the sentence, particularly in discursive writing.

EXAMPLE

The first part of the sentence usually gives the context:

Today, after months of deliberation with its sales network, the German car manufacturer, BMW ...

before revealing the key point or focus of the sentence: *... announced a price increase on all its models.*

If you put the key point first, the sentence gets less interesting as it goes on. Build to your key points – don't throw them away too quickly. Check out your discursive drafts to ensure that you haven't weakened sentences in this way.

How about a diacope?

Pronounced 'dye-ack-o-pee', this is the technical term for something the writer Mark Forsyth has described as 'a verbal sandwich'. This verbal sandwich is a word or phrase repeated after a brief interruption. It is an excellent way to give a final, satisfying close to a passage of dialogue, or to finish a paragraph.

THINGS TO DO AND THINK ABOUT

Over to you ...

Remember that there is no one single way to create a fine piece of writing. All you have found in this book are simply reminders of techniques that will help bring out the best writer in you. Use them to find your own voice. Finding that voice is the essence not only of your success in English but also the basis of forging your own identity. Good luck!

Memorable lines in novels, plays, films, songs often make use of it:

EXAMPLES

I am dying, Egypt, dying.	Shakespeare's 'Antony and Cleopatra'
Game over, man, game over.	The film 'Aliens'
Live, baby live.	INXS
You will, Oscar, you will.	Conversation between painter James Whistler and Oscar Wilde
To be or not to be.	Shakespeare's 'Hamlet'

Is sentence structure all it might be?

You have looked at sentence structure at some length in an earlier section and you know about the importance of sentence variety. But in the white heat of getting an essay or story together, concern about content could blind you to the fact that your sentences might be coming out rather similar in length and construction. Are there too many beginning with the same word? Too many the same length?

Is there an organising principle?

No matter whether you are writing discursively or creatively, always check out your final draft to see if your organising principle is clear to the reader. In other words, is there obviously a strong structure to the piece? Do your ideas flow smoothly and logically from one paragraph or section to the next? Is the transition made smoothly by the use of linking words or phrases? Is there some connection between your opening paragraph and your closing one? In short, have you framed your piece in a way that creates a satisfying shape to the overall presentation?

COMMON MISTAKES TO AVOID

Even if the standard of your English is really quite good, you could find that you have the odd blind spot about certain words or phrases. Although these might not be major mistakes, markers will get a negative view of your technical competence if they happen too often, and your grade could drop. So let's get rid of them right now.

MOST COMMON MISTAKES

Common mistakes	Comment	Example
Accept/except	They can sound the same, but there is a huge difference. 'Accept' is a verb while 'except' is usually seen as a preposition.	*She refused to <u>accept</u> the gift which he gave her.* *She couldn't <u>accept</u> the fact that she had failed the exam.* *He likes all dogs <u>except</u> pugs.*
Alternatives/ options/choices	You can have only two alternatives – if you have more than two choices, you call them options. If in doubt, use 'choices'.	
Apostrophes and plurals	There's a lot of confusion here! Just because a plural word ends in 's' doesn't mean that there has to be an apostrophe lurking around somewhere. (See page 10 for using apostrophes.) If you are simply talking about more than one person or thing, make life easy for yourself. Just add an 's'and leave it at that.	
Bored of/with	One is more formal than the other. 'Bored of' belongs in conversational and informal English while more formal, discursive writing requires 'bored with'.	*She is bored <u>with</u> constantly applying for permission to...* *He's bored <u>of</u> this programme...*
Could have/would have/ should have	When we shorten these pairs of words, they need to be spelled as they are in the column next to this one. Because of the sound the shortened versions make, some people think the '-ve' sound should be written as 'of'. Wrong! 'Of' in these phrases is never correct.	*could've ...* *would've ...* *should've ...*
Dangling modifiers	You might be using these more than you think! These happen when the modifier (or descriptive phrase) gets detached from the word it is intended to modify (or describe). For example: *I saw a dead badger driving down our lane.* Question: who was doing the driving? You or the dead badger? Dead badgers do not usually drive, so presumably it was you. But the 'I' and the 'driving down the lane' have got separated so that the 'driving down the lane' has been left **dangling** at the end of the sentence, **instead of being placed next to the person on whom the sentence focuses.**	It should read: *<u>Driving down our lane, I</u> saw a dead badger.* or *<u>While driving down our lane, I</u> saw a dead badger.*
Different from/to/than	'Different from' is best for formal writing. 'Different to' tends to be more conversational. 'Different than' is more American than English.	*Her attitude is very <u>different from</u> that of her brother...* *Their hamburger is a lot <u>different to</u> McDonalds' ...*
Due to/owing to	Modern English doesn't make a big fuss about which of these you should use. It is, however, generally accepted that 'owing to' is the one for more formal, serious circumstances.	*<u>Owing to</u> a grave illness ...* *<u>Due to</u> a silly mistake ...*
Fewer/less	If you can count them, it's 'fewer': **people, gallons, computers, raisins**. If you can't count them it's 'less': **trouble, flour, petrol, sympathy**.	*<u>Fewer</u> people are watching television these days.* *We use far <u>less</u> petrol with this new car.*

Common mistakes	Comment	Example
Its/it's	**It's** is simply short for 'it is'. Here's a tip: when in doubt, ask yourself this question: If I said 'it is' here, **would it make sense?** For example, would you say: *my dog has hurt it is (it's) paw?* Obviously not – so it must be: *my dog has hurt **its** paw.* Use this as a test if you are ever in doubt.	Always remember: It's = it is If 'it is' makes no sense in your sentence, it cannot be it's – it must be its: *It's a fine day.* *It's a boy!* but *Its ink costs a fortune.* *Put it in its place!*
There/their/they're	When 'there' is the opposite of 'here' or in the phrase 'There is ...' we need the straightforward **there**. When it is a question of ownership or possession, we need **their**. When we are simply shortening they are, we use **they're**. The apostrophe here, as in **'it's'**, is to mark that a letter has been missed out.	*The ball landed over there.* *There is no reason to question this.* but *Their house cost a fortune.* *We met their parents.* and *They're not coming because they're short of time.*
who's/whose	As in words like 'it's' and 'can't', the apostrophe in 'who's' is there to signal a missing letter: it's just short for 'who is'. So when in doubt, ask yourself: could I say 'who is' here? Would it make sense? If you answer 'yes' then use it. If the answer is 'no' then don't. 'Whose' is the possessive (belonging to) of 'who' or 'which' when used as an adjective. But the easiest way to decide when in doubt is to ask yourself: is this short for 'who is' or not?	*Who's up for a game?* *Who's going to believe that?* *She's the girl whose project won.* *It's an idea whose time has come.*

ACTIVITY 1

GETTING IT RIGHT!

Mark each of the following sentences as either correct or incorrect. Where you feel the example is incorrect, write out the sentence correctly as you think appropriate.

1. I disturbed a rat sorting a puncture on my bike tire.

2. Its not surprising that they're not coming.

3. It's typical of her. She could of let us know.

4. Accept for Frieda, everyone accepted there invitation.

5. In the 90s, Abbotsford had less visitors than it has today.

6. We have three alternatives: stay, go or complain to the boss.

7. Due to a serious software malfunction, the bank's ATMs were out of action for 24 hours.

8. The new Audi TT is not that much different from the old one.

9. Looking through my binoculars, the Eiffel Tower loomed above us.

10. Please read over the application form which is enclosed with your family.

11. Their is no point in inviting them. Its not there kind of party.

12. I get less mileage per gallon from this car than I did with the old one.

13. Scotland now has fewer air bases than it did a few years ago.

14. When a horse damages it's leg in a race, its really serious.

15. My gran bought a parrot for my sister named Ebenezer.

16. Series Three is totally different than last years series.

17. For sale: pre-Colombian statue belonging to a student going abroad with curiously carved head.

18. It's too late for they're apology.

19. You should've gone, they would of been delighted to see you.

20. We had less phone calls about the job than we had expected.

PUNCTUATION

Activity 1 – insert full stops and commas

1. Don't get me started on Tim. He's lazy, thoughtless and uses people. Admittedly, his parents, both doctors with Oxfam, have left him to his own devices for most of his life.

2. Having completed his university degree, Liam was looking around for a new job, one that offered him a chance to travel, to make some money and enjoy life. He had, after all, had a pretty grim time so far.

3. Given their lack of experience in house-painting, gardening and plumbing, I wondered if they would be up to the job of converting, not say reconstructing, the old barn. Time alone would tell.

4. 'Well, Missy, is this the best you can do? I've waited hours for you to finish. There's a definite limit to my patience, you know.'

5. Turn left at the Wellington statue. Go straight on until the traffic lights. Provided the traffic is not too bad, try to turn right into Eton Crescent where, all things being equal, I'll be waiting with Ken.

6. Bored to tears by the play, Susie, not the most patient of people at the best of times, decided that she would leave at the first interval.

7. J.C. Bach, son of the great J.S. Bach, spent a fair amount of his creative life in London where, adored by the British public, he enjoyed great financial, artistic and social success.

8. Seeing there was no way out of the barbecue, Sinead and Amy, daughters of our hosts, decided that the time had come to liven things up. Well, that was how they saw it.

9. As you can see, it will take a few days, weeks even, to sort out this mess. Darren is really the limit. He lives in a total shambles.

10. She wondered if they would arrive in time for the meal which, modest though it was, she had spent hours preparing. Cooking, she decided, was not her strong point.

Activity 2 – put the full stops and commas back

The most appealing aspect of the Austro-Hungarian Empire, at least in retrospect, was its European cosmopolitanism. It had few black, brown or yellow subjects, but it contained within itself half the peoples of Europe. It was multi-ethnic, multi-lingual, multi-faith, bound together only, whether willingly or unwillingly, by the imperial discipline. It was closer to the European community of the twenty-first century than to the British Empire of the nineteenth, and possesses still, at least for romantics like me, a fragrant sense of might-have-been.

Activity 3 – insert question marks, exclamation marks, apostrophes, colons and semi-colons

1. How had she got herself into this mess? Who could she turn to now that Pierre's friendly presence had disappeared? Her situation was grim: she knew no one in Vallauris and her money had mostly gone.

2. 'Don't you dare apologise! You think you're so clever, don't you? You have taken advantage of your friends' generosity, every single one of them. Get out!'

3. The night had come down: the streets were deserted, the pavements glistened under the rain and the moon was making a timid appearance.

4. He looked round the room and they were all there: Pam with her eager-beaver eyes locked on John's; Michael looking bored as he slouched in the room's only comfortable chair; Penny, bless her, absorbed totally in the meal's preparation.

5. It was Cheryl who saw her first: a wet, bedraggled figure who, it appeared, was only being held up by the lamp-post's good-will. I wondered if she had eaten at all that day.

6. Looking at all the sketches' signatures, I could see they were all by one hand; (or full stop) the name, however, I could not quite make out.

7. If she's looking for her money's worth, she has certainly chosen the right place: jeans, tops and shoes are all marked at half price.

8. What's the matter? You're not hurt, are you? For heaven's sake, Leslie, say something! Why don't you answer me?

9. Mary, the twins' mother, has been a member of the yoga club's management committee for several years now; (or full stop) no one quite knows why she takes her children's interests so much to heart.

10. I couldn't understand why the women's outing had been set for New Year's Eve; (or full stop) it wasn't really an ideal evening for anyone. Surely the ladies' husbands would have something to say about this?

Activity 4 – add the missing quotation marks

1. 'Look, Sarah, it's high time you made a decision,' fumed her mother. (or exclamation mark in place of comma after 'decision')

2. According to her press agent, she was 'too exhausted to perform'. Some exhaustion! We saw her in the club later that night.

3. 'Strictly Come Dancing' and 'The X-Factor' are forever fighting it out to gain top place in Saturday night audience ratings.

4. 'Are you,' she said, 'available for supper on Tuesday?'

5. This 'saviour' turned out to be nothing but a crook; (or full stop) he left with £50 in his pocket and the boiler still didn't work.

6. 'Mother, mother, I am so happy!' whispered the girl, burying her face in the lap of the faded, tired-looking woman who, with back turned to the shrill intrusive light, was sitting in the one armchair that their dingy sitting room contained. 'I am so happy!' she repeated, 'and you must be happy too!'

This extract is taken from *The Picture of Dorian Gray* by Oscar Wilde.

Activity 5 – how much have you remembered?

1. True   2. True
3. Incorrect. No capital needed after 'said,'
4. False. It has several uses. Check them out.
5. True   6. True   7. False   8. True
9. False. Titles of plays, films, books and poems require inverted commas; the names of characters in them do not.
10. False. They add interesting but inessential information.

SPELLING

Activity 1 – puzzle it out

1. argument
2. trafficking
3. beginning
4. conceited
5. neighbours
6. heroically
7. marketing
8. ceiling
9. sufficient
10. judgement

Activity 2 – mind the gap

1. beginning
2. judgements/separate/prejudices
3. crucial
4. biased/criticisms
5. resemblance
6. Committee
7. orbiting
8. embarrassment/appearance
9. exaggeration
10. guarantee

Activity 4 – how good an editor are you?

Nitrogen is an <u>element</u> essential to all life, but nitrogen <u>compounds</u> are 'extras' largely produced <u>through</u> energy consumption. Nitrogen oxides <u>affect</u> the nitrogen cycle, and when high-temperature oxidation and chemical conversions form <u>nitrogen</u> dioxide, physical effects are possible. NO2 forms the depressing brown in smog. It irritates our eyes and blurs our <u>environment.</u> In animal studies, NO2 has also been <u>shown</u> to be <u>the</u> most dangerous among the eight <u>nitrogen</u> oxides. Inhaled, NO2 reacts quickly with lung tissue and causes cell injury and cell death. Biochemical experiments indicate that the region of the lung most <u>responsible</u> for respiration, the region bound by the terminal respiratory bronchioles and the alveoli, is most affected by inhaled NO2. Lung injury seems related more to the concentration of NO2 than to the <u>length</u> of exposure, but even small <u>concentrations</u> for less than an hour have caused <u>breathing</u> difficulties for some people.

SENTENCE STRUCTURE

Activity 1 – name that sentence

1. Simple
2. Compound
3. Complex
4. Minor
5. Compound
6. Complex
7. Minor
8. Complex
9. Complex
10. Rhetorical question

Activity 3 – create more complex sentences

1. Since the dog knew his scent would be difficult to follow in the water, he raced towards the wood in which a fast-flowing brook ran.

2. Linda has been studying four hours every night, as in two weeks she has an important exam which will determine whether she goes to college or not.

3. Although Neil did not have much money, he bought the bike which cost £3400.

4. The Dean Bridge, designed by Thomas Telford and opened in 1832, was built by the initiative of Provost John Learmouth who wished to develop his lands on the west side of the gorge.

5. The two longest rivers in France are the Loire, which flows into the Atlantic Ocean, and the Rhone, which flows into the Mediterranaean.

6. Since I need to leave for school around eight, I have to work out at the gym early in the morning, whereas my friend Jack, who is unemployed, has all day to work out.

7. If it rains a lot, it is then my job to put the garden furniture in the garage, unless my mother does it before me.

8. When a fishing boat, which was heading out to sea, saw their distress flares, it sent an urgent message to the lifeboat station.

9. When the baby was five months, she started to crawl whenever she had an audience.

10. A serious accident which involved the London train and a local goods train occurred on Sunday near Longniddry.

Activity 5 – sentences that create atmosphere

It was a convivial and noisy occasion, with everyone sitting at three trestle tables, which were covered in long white cloths, and shouting to one another in all directions about market matters, while half a dozen girls passed in and out bearing platters of beef and pork, tureens of soup, basins of vegetables on wide trays. Although I did not think I knew a soul in the room and felt somewhat out of place especially in my funeral garb among the tweed and corduroy, I nevertheless enjoyed myself greatly.

Activity 6 – better sentence management

Our latest publication project involves a study of the novel. This will look at its origins, its evolution through the centuries and some modern day treatments of it. We shall also examine whether the scope envisaged is too broad and whether it can be completed in 25 000 words. Finally, it will examine how the project should be handled if it is felt our time would be better spent on a more focused approach.

WORKING WITH PARAGRAPHS

Activity 1 – find the missing link

(1) on the other hand (2) nevertheless (3) Despite/in spite of (4) For instance/example (5) thus (6) In spite of/despite

Activity 2 – expand notes into a paragraph

Answers might vary. The following is only one of many possibilities.

Messages from Ankara report that a catastrophic earthquake has occurred in north-western Turkey. This has been particularly violent in the Izmit region where the town has been completely destroyed. As a result, thousands of people are now homeless and the death toll is estimated at more than 17 000. While the Turkish government is sending thousands troops and transport to help, rescue work is being hampered by torrential rain and floods. The news has aroused world-wide sympathy, which has led to food, water, clothing and medical supplies being flown in. Offers of help have already been received from twelve countries.

Activity 3 – link the sentences

Answers might vary. The following is only one of many possibilities.

In 2008, five years after the success of *Buddha Da*, Anne Donovan published her second novel, *Being Emily*. Here the focus was also on a close-knit Glasgow family. This time, it was seen, not from the multiple perspectives of the earlier novel, but from viewpoint of a single narrator, Fiona O'Connell, whom we first meet as a second-year pupil at a comprehensive school. The novel takes the form of a *bildungsroman*. This a novel in which we watch the hero/heroine coming of age, frequently making mistakes in the process. By the novel's end, Fiona is a married woman, expecting her first baby, installed once again in the flat where the story begins. In the years between, Fiona and her family suffer upsets which test their initial solidarity before harmony is finally restored.

Activity 4 – restore the paragraphs

Paragraph 1	A recent issue of …
Paragraph 2	The list is all important.
Paragraph 3	So the most important …
Paragraph 4	Some years ago …
Paragraph 5	Direct mail is the most …

Activity 5 – build a paragraph (1)

(4) In Egypt, the landscape has been changing for centuries, some might say for thousands of years. (7) The most significant of these changes have undoubtedly been those affecting the Nile River basin. (2) In this particular river basin, there is now year-round irrigation of the soil rather than reliance, as once, on the river's annual flood. (1) This conversion to continuous irrigation has led to significantly increased agricultural production. (3) In turn, this has contributed to a substantial increase in the basin's population. (5) As a result of the growing numbers and their associated activities, the prosperity of the basin has grown steadily over the centuries. (6) Boosting the increasing wealth of this region still more was the project to build in 1960 the Aswan High Dam, an undertaking worthy of the pharaohs themselves.

Activity 6 – build a paragraph (2)

It is all very well to say that fracking in our own backyard frees us from the uncertainties of international political upheavals, but what of the cost to the Earth's crust? This is a cost which has gone largely ignored by profit-hungry capitalists who minimise any question of the risk of earth tremors. But no less a journal than *Science Today* has underlined these risks, citing mid-sized tremors in Colorado, Texas, Japan and Sumatra. Commenting on these tremors, the paper's author, Helen Savage remarks:

'If the small number of earthquakes increases, it could indicate that faults are becoming critically stressed and might soon host a larger earthquake'.

So much for earth tremors, but what of a second cause for concern: the dangers to aquifers (the name given to underground channels carrying water) which drilling can bring? According to Tom Myers, a Reno-based researcher, writing in *Ground Water*, chemically treated drilling fluid can migrate through thousands of feet of rock and endanger water supplies in as little as three years. Imagine the disaster which contaminated water supplies could bring if the respected Myers is to be believed. Furthermore, if these drilled wells are not properly capped, harmful methane gas may escape, adding to already grave greenhouse-gas worries. Various studies by universities, governments and industry have determined that methane leakage can amount to almost 12 per cent of natural gas produced each year. For all these reasons, it is surely high time that the world's nations came together to investigate the current damage that is being wreaked on the Earth's crust. But the dangers below the ground are worryingly mirrored in dangers above the ground as well.

DEVELOPING VOCABULARY

Activity 1 – substitute a word from the Latin prefixes grid

1. circumvent
2. adjacent
3. abduct(ed)
4. ambivalent
5. multifaceted
6. coalesce(d)
7. antecedents
8. subordinate
9. extrasensory
10. premeditate(d)

Activity 2 – find, substitute and rewrite (Latin)

1. prelude
2. antediluvian
3. coalition
4. contraband
5. advent
6. ultramarine
7. ambidextrous
8. circumspect
9. translucent
10. suburban

Sentences will vary but the following might be useful guidelines:

1. The cocktail party was a prelude to the conference itself.
2. His clothes are positively antediluvian; they look as though they came out of the Ark!
3. The two parties formed a coalition in order to defeat their main political rival.
4. The coastguard had been watching out for contraband coming in on luxury yachts.
5. Since the advent of spell-checks on computers, spelling has improved in general.
6. She arrived in an ultramarine Elie Saab outfit. Fabulous!
7. Breaking his right wrist just before the exam was not the end of the world since he is ambidextrous.
8. He's incredibly circumspect; he's forever looking out for potential risks to his fortune.
9. I need some privacy, but remember the door has to be translucent if I'm to see what I'm doing.
10. She's such a city creature, I can't imagine her living in a suburban flat.

Activity 3 – substitute a word from the Greek prefixes grid

1. amphibious
2. paramedic
3. synagogue
4. hyperbole
5. peripatetic
6. synonym
7. hypothermia
8. dialect
9. anaemia
10. metamorphosis

Activity 4 – find, substitute and rewrite (Greek)

Sentences will vary but the following might be useful guidelines:

1. This is an illness endemic to the Eritrean region.
2. This is a statement which at first appears to be a paradox.
3. We need to synchronize our watches./We need to check our watches are synchronized.
4. A periscope is a handy instrument in a submarine.
5. We need a hypodermic for the serum.
6. His book is a diachronic study of the development of medicine.
7. It is currently a national dystopia.
8. They have formed a syndicate to own the racehorse.
9. Atlantis was thought to have disappeared into the depths of the ocean as a result of an unprecedented volcanic cataclysm.
10. He has a slow metabolism.

Activity 5 – apply your knowledge of prefixes

1. 'amoral' – without morals, not acknowledging usual concepts of right or wrong; for this person, morality does not exist.
   'immoral' – not **following** accepted standards of morality, although aware probably of what these standards are.